Lessons for Education from COVID-19

A POLICY MAKER'S HANDBOOK FOR MORE RESILIENT SYSTEMS

This work is published under the responsibility of the Secretary-General of the OECD. The opinions expressed and arguments employed herein do not necessarily reflect the official views of OECD member countries.

This document, as well as any data and map included herein, are without prejudice to the status of or sovereignty over any territory, to the delimitation of international frontiers and boundaries and to the name of any territory, city or area.

The statistical data for Israel are supplied by and under the responsibility of the relevant Israeli authorities. The use of such data by the OECD is without prejudice to the status of the Golan Heights, East Jerusalem and Israeli settlements in the West Bank under the terms of international law.

Please cite this publication as:
OECD (2020), *Lessons for Education from COVID-19: A Policy Maker's Handbook for More Resilient Systems*, OECD Publishing, Paris, *https://doi.org/10.1787/0a530888-en*.

ISBN 978-92-64-71826-5 (print)
ISBN 978-92-64-78203-7 (pdf)

Photo credits: Cover © Sasha Chebotarev/Shutterstock.com; 4 PM production/Shutterstock.com; M2020/Shutterstock.com; Valeriya Kozoriz/Shutterstock.com.

Corrigenda to publications may be found on line at: *www.oecd.org/about/publishing/corrigenda.htm*.
© OECD 2020

The use of this work, whether digital or print, is governed by the Terms and Conditions to be found at *http://www.oecd.org/termsandconditions*.

Foreword

Few groups are less vulnerable to COVID-19 than school children, but few groups have been more affected by the policy responses to contain this virus: 1.5 billion students around the world were locked out of their schools, some for more than half a school year. Some of them were able to find their way around closed school doors through alternative learning opportunities, well-supported by their parents and teachers. But many remained shut out when their school shut down, particularly those from the most marginalised groups, who did not have access to digital learning resources, or lacked the support, resilience and engagement to learn on their own.

If anything, this period has made publicly and widely visible the many benefits that students draw from being able to learn in close contact with their teachers and their peers, and with access to the variety of services which schools offer. This public awareness of the importance of schools and of teachers can help promote further engagement and support from communities and parents for schools and for teachers. This is important, as a likely result of the pandemic will be greater financial austerity resulting from the economic adjustment that the health and economic costs of the pandemic will bring about.

But the crisis has also resulted in unprecedented technological and social innovation in education, as learners, parents, educators, the technology sector, and policy makers came together to solve new problems. Perhaps there was less reform in these months, but there has certainly been more change. The crisis has also accelerated policy thinking, changing mind-sets on topics for which there has historically been much resistance to change. The crisis experience has highlighted the role of technology in the future of education, neither to conserve nor simply replace existing practices, but to transform them. It has brought new appreciation for the multi-dimensional function of formal education and reinforced the notion that learning is an activity and not a place. It has refocused attention to the core purpose of assessment as the driver of student and system improvement rather than just a necessary hoop to jump through along a standardised learning pathway. These changing attitudes are the silver linings of a very difficult year; herein we begin to chart our route to a brighter new normal.

However, to transform schooling at scale, we need not just a vision of what is possible, but also smart strategies that help make change. The road of educational reform is littered with good ideas that were poorly implemented. And the laws, regulations, structures and institutions on which educational leaders tend to focus are just like the small visible tip of an iceberg. The reason why it is so hard to move school systems is that there is a much larger invisible part beneath the surface. This invisible part is about the interests, beliefs, motivations and fears of the people who are involved in education, parents and teachers included. This is where unexpected collisions occur, because this part of educational reform tends to evade the radar screen of public policy. That is why educational leaders are rarely successful with reform unless they build a shared understanding and collective ownership for change, and unless they build capacity and create the right policy climate, with accountability measures designed to encourage innovation, rather than compliance.

This handbook explores how policy makers can use the moment of the crisis to leverage change in education as a whole-of-society project. Expecting that the future will continue to surprise us, it discusses how we can make education systems more resilient, helping learners and educators not just to keep the world in balance, but also to live and thrive in an imbalanced world. It examines what policy makers can do to help educators and leaders develop the knowledge and skills to get ready for this. And last but not least it looks at ways in which we can close learning gaps to help everyone realise their potential.

The method of the handbook is simple: it leverages the experience of education systems from around the world. In these times, educators and policy makers need not just look forward, but also outward. The difference between education systems that are open to the world and ready to learn from and with other experiences, and those that feel threatened by being exposed to alternative ways of thinking and working is likely to be a key differentiator in the educational progress that we will see around the world. The world is indifferent to tradition and past reputations, unforgiving of frailty, and ignorant of custom or practice. Success will go to those individuals and nations that are swift to adapt, slow to complain and open to change. The task of governments is to help citizens rise to the challenges.

Andreas Schleicher
Special Advisor on Education Policy to the Secretary-General
Director for Education and Skills
OECD

Acknowledgements

The *Education Policy Outlook,* the OECD's analytical observatory of education policy, is a collaborative effort between OECD countries and economies, the OECD Secretariat, and invited institutions, as well as all actors working within participating education systems to help students achieve their potential.

This report was prepared by members of the Education Policy Outlook team (Christa Rawkins, Diana Toledo Figueroa [Project Leader], Savannah Saunders, Jonathan James and Clément Dumont), under the responsibility of Paulo Santiago, Head of the Policy Advice and Implementation Division, and Andreas Schleicher, Special Advisor on Education Policy to the OECD Secretary-General, and Director for Education and Skills. Nicholas Biddle contributed with comments during the finalisation of the report, as part of his Thomas J. Alexander fellowship with the Education Policy Outlook Team during 2020. Stephen Flynn provided editorial support and Rachel Linden, Sophie Limoges, Alison Burke and Jason Fallow provided communications support.

Sincere thanks are due, particularly in the context of the COVID-19 pandemic, to the many contributors who helped shape the objectives of the work of the OECD Education Policy Outlook during 2020. The Education Policy Outlook National Co-ordinators provided guidance and comments throughout the development of this Handbook, including bilateral exchanges with more than 20 participating education systems to gain a deeper understanding of the key challenges facing policy makers in the second half of 2020, as well as their policy priorities moving forward. This report also benefitted from invited contributions from several projects across the Directorate for Education and Skills: the Higher Education Policy project, the vocational education and training (VET) and Adult Learning project, the Future of Education and Skills 2030 project, the Implementing Education Policies project, the Teachers' Professional Learning study, and the Strength through Diversity project.

The OECD Secretariat is also thankful to all those who took part in the virtual extraordinary *Education Policy Reform Dialogues 2020: Shifting education practices towards a more resilient new normal*, which took place on 26-27 October 2020. This report acted as background documentation to the event, and has since been enriched by key outcomes of delegates' discussions. The event was co-hosted by the OECD and the Department of Education and Training of the Flemish Community of Belgium. It was moderated by Hon. Hekia Parata (former Minister of Education of New Zealand) and brought together over 130 senior policy makers representing 42 registered delegations from OECD member countries, key partners and non-member countries, as well as other international and partner organisations.

Finally, the OECD is also grateful to the European Commission for the financial and analytical collaboration it provided for the updates of 11 Education Policy Outlook Country Policy Profiles from 2017 to 2020. Findings from these policy profiles also contributed to the preparation of this Handbook as part of the wider knowledge base of the Education Policy Outlook.

Table of contents

Foreword	3
Acknowledgements	5
Abbreviations and acronyms	9
Executive summary	11
Introduction	13
Making the case for change: We must drive education into a better normal, now	14
Developing a roadmap: A framework for responsiveness and resilience	15
About this Handbook	16
References	17
1. Education actors should nurture resilient mind-sets that value people and processes over classrooms and devices	19
In Brief	20
Background: Why now?	21
Evidence	22
Policy pointers	35
2. Educators need new skills and new knowledge to capitalise on new education priorities and means of delivery	41
In Brief	42
Background: Why now?	43
Evidence	44
Policy pointers	51
References	53
3. Addressing learning gaps now will minimise disruption in students' educational journeys	55
In Brief	56
Background: Why now?	57
Evidence	58
Policy pointers	65
References	67

4. Annexes: Associated resources for policy makers — 71

- Annex 1. Links to government sources on delivery methods in the second half of 2020 — 72
- Annex 2. Links to governments' main system-level guidelines for the second half of 2020 — 76
- Annex 3. Mapping of elements from governments' system-level guidelines according to the EPO's Framework for Responsiveness and Resilience in education (in process) — 78
- Annex 4. Recent work from the OECD's Future of Education and Skills 2030 project in the context of the COVID-19 pandemic — 80
- Annex 5. Recent work from the OECD's Implementing Education Policies project in the context of the COVID-19 pandemic — 81
- Annex 6. Professional learning policies from the pre-crisis period with evidence of positive impact — 82
- Annex 7. Selected current policy efforts to support professional learning — 89
- Annex 8. Recent work from the OECD's Teachers' Professional Learning Study — 92
- Annex 9. Policies addressing learning gaps from the pre-crisis period with evidence of positive impact — 93
- Annex 10. Selected current policy efforts to address learning gaps — 100
- Annex 11. Recent work from the OECD's Strength through Diversity project in the context of the COVID-19 pandemic — 104

FIGURES

- Figure 1.1. Readiness for ubiquitous learning varies within and between OECD education systems — 23
- Figure 1.2. Delivery methods for the second half of 2020 (primary and secondary education) — 25
- Figure 1.3. Delivery methods for the second half of 2020 (post-secondary education) — 26
- Figure 1.4. Adapting pedagogical practices for the academic term of the second half of 2020 — 29
- Figure 2.1. Certain policy levers for educators' resilience require strengthening across the OECD — 45
- Figure 3.1. Several policy levers for student resilience require strengthening across the OECD — 59

INFOGRAPHICS

- Infographic 1.1. Lesson 1 and policy pointers for action — 20
- Infographic 2.1. Lesson 2 and policy pointers for action — 42
- Infographic 3.1. Lesson 3 and policy pointers for action — 56

TABLES

- Table 2.1. Professional learning policies from the pre-crisis period with evidence of positive impact — 47
- Table 2.2. Promising policy initiatives for professional learning implemented in 2020 — 49
- Table 3.1. Pre-crisis policy examples to address learning gaps with evidence of positive impact — 61
- Table 3.2. Promising policy initiatives to address learning gaps implemented in 2020 — 63
- Table 4.1. Sources consulted for information about delivery methods in the second half of 2020 — 72
- Table 4.2. System-level guidelines consulted for information about shifting pedagogical practices in the second half of 2020 — 76
- Table 4.3. Classification of information collected through system-level guidelines — 78

Abbreviations and acronyms

ASQA Australian Skills Authority (Australia)

BMBF Federal Ministry of Education and Research (*Bundesministerium für Bildung und Forschung*, Germany)

BMBWF Federal Ministry of Education, Science and Research (*Bundesministerium für Bildung, Wissenschaft und Forschung*, Austria)

CNED National Centre for Distance Education (*Centre National d'Enseignement à Distance*, France)

CAP Professional Vocational Education Track (*Certificat d'Aptitude Professionnelle*, France)

CEDEFOP The European Centre for the Development of Vocational Training (Greece)

CFAE School Association Professional Development Centres (*Centros de Formação de Associação de Escolas*, Portugal)

CPD Continued Professional Development

CSL The Centre for School Leadership (Ireland)

CoLs New Zealand introduced Communities of Learning | *Kāhui Ako* (New Zealand)

DES Department of Education and Skills (Ireland)

DEIS Delivering Equality of Opportunity in Schools (Ireland)

DIA The Comprehensive Assessment of Learning, (*Diagnóstico Integral de Aprendizajes*, Chile)

ECEC Early Childhood Education and Care

EDUFI Finnish National Agency for Education (*Opetushallitus Utbildningsstyrelsen*, Finland)

EPO Education Policy Outlook

ESF European Social Fund

FINEEC The Finnish Education Evaluation Centre (*Kansallinen koulutuksen arviointikeskus*, Finland)

FCNM Framework Convention for the Protection of National Minorities (France)

GDP Gross Domestic Product

HEIs Higher Education Institutions

HEPPP Higher Education Participation and Partnerships Programme (Australia)

KS Norwegian Association of Local and Regional Authorities (Norway)

LTO Long-term Occasional Teachers (Ontario (Canada))

MEXT Ministry of Education, Culture, Sports, Science and Technology (Japan)

MOOC Massive Open Online Course

MINEDUC Ministry of Education (Ministerio de Educación, Chile)

NIFU Norwegian Research Institute (*Nordisk institutt for studier av innovasjon, forskning og utdanning*, Norway)

NTIP The New Teacher Induction Program (Ontario (Canada))

NZQA New Zealand Qualifications Authority (New Zealand)

OKM Ministry of Education and Culture (*Opetus- ja kulttuuriministeriö*, Finland)

PISA Programme for International Student Assessment

PNPSE National Programme to Promote Educational Success (*Plano Nacional de Promoção do Sucesso Escolar*, Portugal)

SEP Preferential School Subsidy (*Ley de Subvención Escolar Preferencial*, Chile)

TALIS Teaching and Learning International Survey

TEIP3 Third Generation of the Education Territories of Priority Intervention Programme (*Territórios Educativos de Intervenção Prioritária*, Portugal)

TEQSA Tertiary Education Quality and Standards Agency (Australia)

TPL Teacher Professional Learning

VET Vocational Education and Training

VIVE The National Research and Analysis Centre for Welfare (*Det Nationale Forskinings-og Analysecenter For Velfaerd*, Denmark)

YÖK Council of Higher Education (*Yükseköğretim Kurulu*, Turkey)

Executive summary

We need to act now

For all those currently in the education system, the COVID-19 crisis marks a critical moment in students' learning pathways, with potential implications well beyond the crisis. Widespread institutional closures and subsequent estimated learning losses, as well as continued disruption as institutions begin welcoming students back under new constraints, are likely to have a significant educational and economic impact on individuals and societies for years to come. This means that merely returning education to the status quo of the old normal, which was already failing to meet the needs of all learners, is not an option. Policy makers must therefore support all actors across the education system to maintain the momentum of collective emergency action and leap forward into a better normal.

We know what to do

Three insights emerge from the crisis as launch pads from which to make such a leap. Firstly, institutional closures and emergency efforts for educational continuity have made it clear that learning does not need to be constricted within the four walls of an educational institution, but, with the right relationships and mind-sets in place, can occur anywhere and at any time. Secondly, the crisis has revealed that education systems are not too heavy to move and, although it is challenging, it is possible for education actors to reach agreements that can make significant change happen in education. Finally, the crisis has emphasised that only resilient education systems that plan for disruption, and that withstand and recover from adverse events, will be able to fulfil the fundamental human right to education, whatever the circumstances, and foster the level of human capital required for successful economies and societies.

Today's education systems therefore face the critical task of balancing the crisis-induced *urgent* challenge of building greater **resilience** and the *important* challenge of increasing **responsiveness** to the changing needs of learners in a post-industrial society. But what are resilience and responsiveness in education? Throughout 2020, the Education Policy Outlook (EPO) has been drawing on insights from a decade of policy analysis, as well as other relevant OECD work and ongoing collaborations with over 40 participating education systems, to develop a Framework for Responsiveness and Resilience in education.

This Handbook carries that work forward, adapting it to the specific needs of education systems organising the academic term of the second half of 2020 in the context of an ongoing pandemic to continue supporting countries in 2021 and beyond. The Handbook is based on analysis of international thematic evidence, selected pre-crisis policies with evidence of progress towards stated objectives, and relevant promising initiatives currently being implemented in participating education systems, as well as exchanges with countries participating in the activities of the Education Policy Outlook. In addition to these bilateral exchanges, this Handbook also integrates highlights of discussions at the *Education Policy Reform Dialogues 2020: Shifting education practices towards a more resilient new normal*, which took place virtually on 26-27 October 2020, for which an earlier version of this report acted as background document for the event.

How can we do it?

The Handbook proposes three key lessons for policy makers, each relating to key policy priorities for the current academic year, as identified in bilateral meetings with over 20 participating education systems in 2020 (see below).

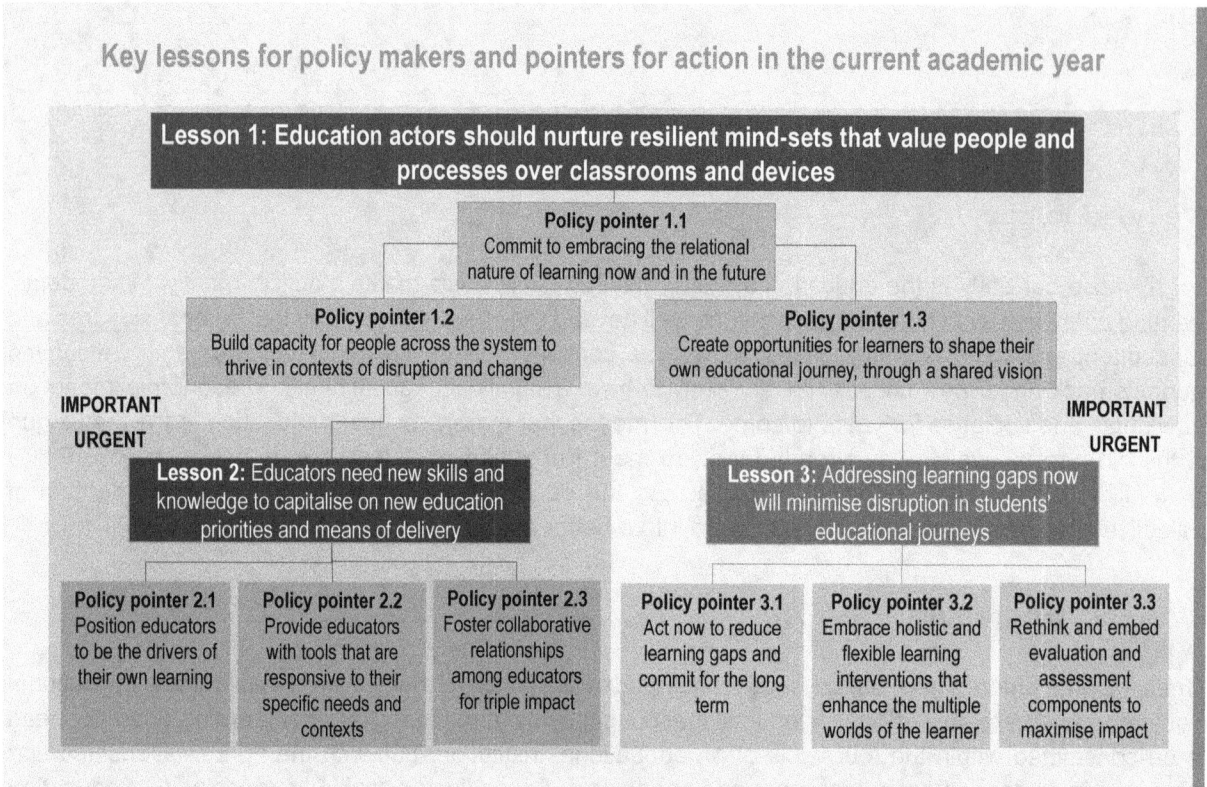

Key lessons for policy makers and pointers for action in the current academic year

Lesson one calls on education systems to capitalise upon the full spectrum of different modes of educational delivery by nurturing resilient mind-sets that value people and processes over classrooms and devices. Analysis of the system-level guidelines in place and the current delivery modes adopted across participating education systems indicates that some new remote modes of delivery prevail, even as institutions reopen, and that, to support this, many countries are working to adapt pedagogical practices in areas such as personalised and flexible learning and building digital capacity. However, countries need to embrace the opportunity to move beyond a binary model of education (online or offline) towards an approach which effectively harnesses learning in all its guises. This will require developing partnerships with a wider variety of actors beyond the education institution, building human capacity for change, and empowering learners to shape their own learning, through a shared vision across an education system.

Lesson two grows out of lesson one, investigating more deeply how policy makers can effectively support educators to gain the new knowledge and skills they need for a better normal. Analysis reveals that carefully designed policy processes relating to professional learning can combine both the key policy components of effective professional development (content focus, sustained duration, school-embeddedness, and active learning and collaboration) with key policy levers for educator resilience and responsiveness (well-being, collaboration and leadership of learning).

Lesson three also takes a deeper dive into aspects of lesson one, exploring approaches to the urgent task of addressing learning gaps exacerbated by crisis. Analysis reveals policy approaches that combine both the key policy components of effective learning interventions (personalised learning, additional or specialised instruction and targeted additional resources) with key policy levers for student resilience and responsiveness (well-being, evaluation and assessment, capacity building, and home-school link.

Introduction

About this section: With the crisis facing global society today in the context of the COVID-19 pandemic, key lessons must be retained, in order to tackle old, new and future broader challenges. This section provides the background for this report, briefly outlining the broader rational for change. It also provides an overview of the process that the OECD Education Policy Outlook is following during 2020-21 to develop an actionable framework for Responsiveness and Resilience in education, that supports countries to balance the urgent and the important as a mutually reinforcing endeavour for the medium and longer term.

Making the case for change: We must drive education into a better normal, now

The COVID-19 crisis undoubtedly marks a critical moment in students' education pathways, with varying implications for their emotional, social and economic well-being. At its peak during the first half of 2020, in an effort to contain the virus, around 91% of the world's enrolled learners were shut out of their usual place of learning (UNESCO, 2020[1]). The OECD estimates that, by June 2020, 80% of member and partner countries had already employed some degree of school closure for more than three months, around one-third of the average academic year (OECD, 2020[2]). For the current student cohort, if education systems are unable to make up the equivalent learning loss, this could result in 3% lower career earnings; for the typical nation, this could result in around 1.5% lower Gross Domestic Product (GDP) throughout the remainder of the century (Hanushek and Woessmann, 2020[3]).

The world economy has also fallen into the deepest recession since the Second World War, with young workers predicted to be among those the hardest hit. Re-connecting young people with the labour market can be very challenging once they lose touch with it. Following the global financial crisis, it took a decade for youth unemployment rates to return to pre-crisis levels (OECD, 2020[4]). Therefore, today's learners not only face tougher educational trajectories due to possible learning loss, but also potentially fewer opportunities in the labour market for many years to come.

At the same time, the COVID-19 crisis increasingly reveals itself to be not simply a pandemic, but rather a *syndemic*. This means that social factors play at least as strong a role in the spread and impact of the virus as biological factors; an integrated approach that reaches beyond clinical medicine and public health is therefore necessary. A broader vision encompassing, for example, education, employment, basic living conditions or environment is more likely to succeed in strengthening global resilience against this virus (Horton, 2020[5]).

All of this means that merely aiming to return education to the pre-COVID-19 status quo is not an option. The unprecedented challenges facing this generation and global society in general demand that education systems maintain the momentum of collective emergency action to leap forward into a better normal. Emergency measures imposed by the crisis have planted the seeds of such a transition; in order for the roots to take hold, new knowledge must now translate into action. This does not necessarily mean reinventing the wheel, but steering it in the direction of brighter destinations for societies. Looking forward, today's learners deserve education systems that embrace student inclusion to ensure that all individuals thrive, that reconfigure curriculum and assessment to recognise the full complexities of thinking and doing, and that value and empower educators as advanced knowledge workers operating in collegial work structures, accountable to both their peers and key stakeholders. Policy makers must now act smartly, identifying the levers of change where quick wins today can translate into greater wins tomorrow.

Throughout 2020, the Education Policy Outlook (EPO) has been investigating what form such smart action could take. Since February, drawing on insights from a decade of policy analysis, as well as other relevant OECD work, the EPO has been developing a Framework for Responsiveness and Resilience in education based on analysis of international evidence and its knowledge base of education policy practices in over 40 education systems. Country-specific analysis undertaken for 12 EPO Country Policy Profiles published in 2020 also provided an overview of system preparedness for the COVID-19 crisis in individual education systems, and insight into initial responses. Complementing this, between July and September 2020, the EPO held bilateral exchanges with over 20 participating education systems to gain a deeper understanding of key challenges facing policy makers in the second half of 2020 and their policy priorities moving forward. An earlier version of this report also served as the main background document of the *Education Policy Reform Dialogues 2020: Shifting education practices towards a more resilient new normal*. This Handbook integrates highlights of these discussions.

Developing a roadmap: A framework for responsiveness and resilience

Education systems operate in a world that is constantly evolving towards new equilibria, but short-term crises disrupt, accelerate or divert longer-term evolutions. Balancing the urgent and the important thus emerges as the key everyday task of education systems.

Today's education systems — mostly designed for the industrial era — face the *important* challenge of transitioning to a post-industrial society. This demands greater **responsiveness** to increasingly diverse populations, changing labour markets, well-being aspects, and the breadth of skills and knowledge that individuals need to thrive. Education systems also face the *urgent* challenge of absorbing and adapting to the disruption of not just the COVID-19 crisis, but also other crises as they continue to emerge around the world (e.g. natural disasters, but also social, political or economic disruptions). This requires building **resilience**, seizing the opportunity to learn from this crisis, and future ones, in order to inform longer-term improvement (Hynes, Linkov and Trump, 2020[6]). To help education systems address the urgent and the important not as competing priorities but as a mutually reinforcing endeavour for the medium and longer term, during 2020-2021, the EPO is developing an actionable Framework for Responsiveness and Resilience (see below).

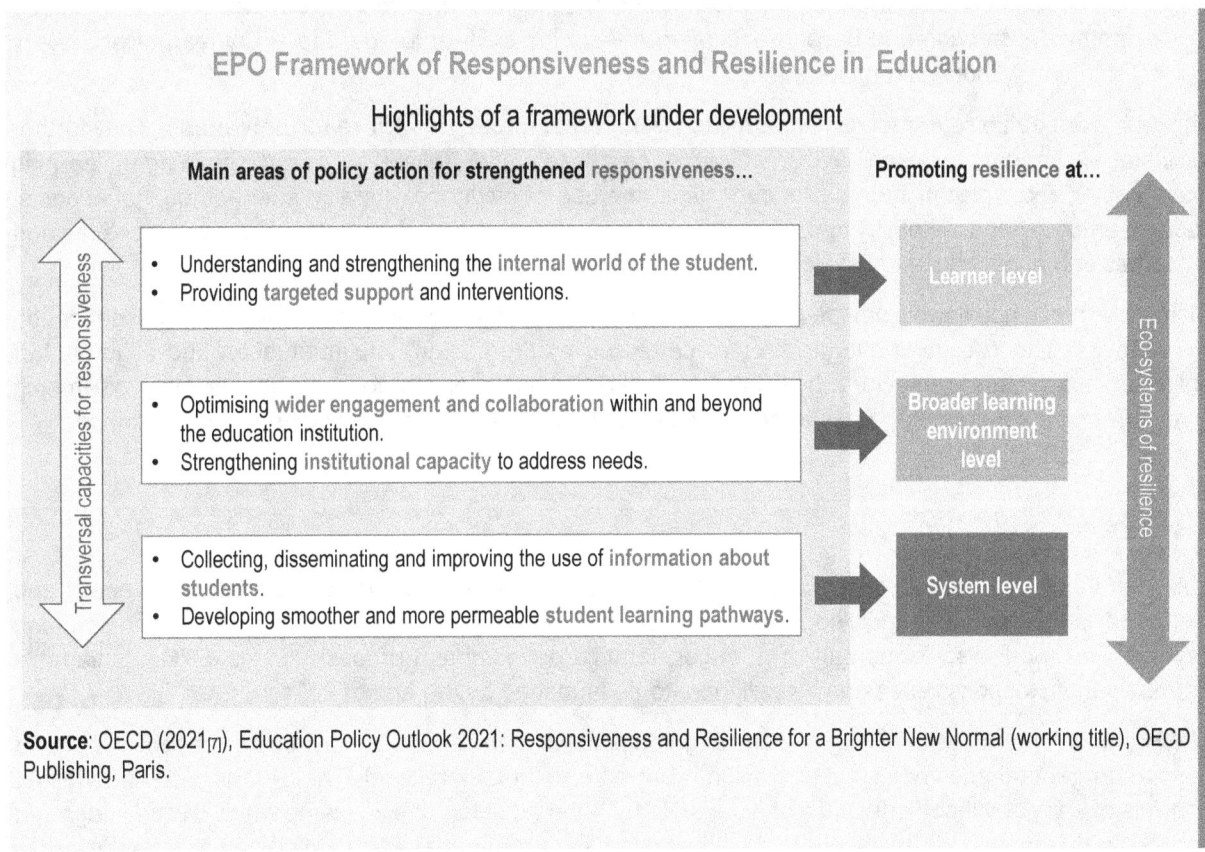

Source: OECD (2021[7]), Education Policy Outlook 2021: Responsiveness and Resilience for a Brighter New Normal (working title), OECD Publishing, Paris.

According to this framework under development, education systems need to develop into responsive eco-systems that promote resilience at different levels. These policy eco-systems facilitate greater coherence between policy priorities, systemic context and key actors. They bring together policies at different moments of their lifecycles (such as in their design, implementation, consolidation or evaluation), and with different scopes of action (such as education level, territorial coverage and target audience, among others), to increase synergies between them. The key elements of these eco-systems interact constantly, but can be conceptualised as follows:

- **Resilient learners** adjust positively to change, manage uncertainty, and respond to shocks. This starts with the student's internal world, including emotional well-being, self-efficacy, critical thinking and growth mind-set (Chernyshenko, Kankaraš and Drasgow, 2018[8]). Education systems must equip learners with such skills and adapt educational experiences to their individual interests, abilities, aspirations, and backgrounds through more personalised or targeted approaches. This is particularly important for those in adverse circumstances (Pigozzi, 2020[9]; Burde et al., 2016[10]).
- A **resilient broader learning environment** drives learner and system resilience. Educational institutions contribute when they are at the centre of a network of co-ordinated supports that sustain well-being (Ungar, 2011[11]; Reyes, 2013[12]). Establishing a resilient broader learning environment implies bringing together a variety of actors within and between different learning environments, both inside and outside the education institution, for effective synergies. Such an approach can also empower all related actors to implement policies that respond to local contexts.
- **Resilient systems** 'bounce forward' rather than simply 'bounce back' (Hynes, Linkov and Trump, 2020[6]). They are dynamic enough to fulfil every student's needs- even in changing contexts- and so must learn with the learner, evolving in synchrony with societies' future needs. The capacity to collect information about education contexts and learners, building a richer picture of their needs and progress, is therefore essential. Similarly, flexible and more permeable transitions and pathways through and beyond education enable the system to adapt to every learner and every situation without disruption.

This framework also contemplates other **more transversal capacities for responsiveness**. They further facilitate exchanges between levels, enhance processes and deliver new and meaningful learning experiences. Examples include digital capacities, the use of evidence, but also socio-emotional aspects, such as empathy and the ability to develop interconnections and shared understandings of processes and outcomes in a given education system.

Ultimately, resilience flows from the practices, people, processes and tools that shape learners' education experiences. These components are in turn catalysed by the design, implementation and alignment of policies. Through this Framework, the Education Policy Outlook supports policy makers at this over-arching level, offering a coherent approach to policy work that fosters greater responsiveness and resilience.

About this Handbook

This Handbook is a product of the overall work undertaken by the EPO in 2020 on responsiveness and resilience to leverage that knowledge base to support policy makers in the context of the pandemic and beyond. This work also forms part of a longer iterative development process for the EPO's actionable Framework of Responsiveness and Resilience, to be launched by the end of 2021.

The Handbook proposes three key lessons to guide policymakers' efforts in the current academic year and beyond, in general and vocational education, from primary to tertiary level. The EPO is also undertaking analysis of early childhood education and care (ECEC) and adult learning systems which will be integrated into the final Framework. Lesson one (Education actors should nurture resilient mind-sets that value people and processes over classrooms and devices) is the over-arching lesson. It is supported by Lesson two (Educators need new skills and new knowledge to capitalise on new education priorities and means of delivery) and Lesson three (Addressing learning gaps now will minimise disruption in students' educational journeys). Each lesson draws on recent OECD work and other international evidence, successful pre-crisis policies, and current promising policy efforts. This informs practical policy pointers for action

References

Chernyshenko, O., M. Kankaraš and F. Drasgow (2018), "Social and emotional skills for student success and well-being: Conceptual framework for the OECD study on social and emotional skills", *OECD Education Working Papers*, No. 173, OECD Publishing, Paris, https://dx.doi.org/10.1787/db1d8e59-en. [8]

Elsevier (ed.) (2016), "Education in emergencies: A review of theory and research", *Review of Educational Research*, Vol. 87/3, pp. 619-658, https://doi.org/10.3102%2F0034654316671594 (accessed on 13 October 2020). [10]

Hanushek, E. and L. Woessmann (2020), "The economic impacts of learning losses", *OECD Education Working Papers*, No. 225, OECD Publishing, Paris, https://dx.doi.org/10.1787/21908d74-en. [3]

Horton, R. (2020), *Offline: COVID-19 is not a pandemic*, Elsevier, Amsterdam, p. 874, https://doi.org/10.1016/S0140-6736(20)32000-6. [5]

Hynes, W., I. Linkov and B. Trump (2020), "A Systemic Approach to Dealing with Covid-19 and Future Shocks", *New Approaches to Economic Challenges (NAEC)*, OECD Publications, Paris, http://www.oecd.org/naec/projects/resilience/NAEC_Resilience_and_Covid19.pdf (accessed on 13 October 2020). [6]

OECD (2021), *Education Policy Outlook 2021: Responsiveness and Resilience for a Brighter New Normal (working title)*. [7]

OECD (2020), *Education at a Glance 2020: OECD Indicators*, OECD Publishing, Paris, https://dx.doi.org/10.1787/69096873-en. [2]

OECD (2020), *OECD Employment Outlook 2020: Worker Security and the COVID-19 Crisis*, OECD Publishing, Paris, https://dx.doi.org/10.1787/1686c758-en. [4]

Pigozzi, M. (2020), "Education in Emergencies and for Reconstruction: A Developmental Approach", *Education Working Papers*, UNICEF Publications, New York, https://bettercarenetwork.org/sites/default/files/attachments/Education%20in%20Emergencies%20and%20for%20Reconstruction.pdf (accessed on 13 October 2020). [9]

Reyes, J. (2013), "What Matters Most for Education Resilience : A Framework Paper", *Education Working Paper (Numbered Series)*, No. 78811, World Bank Publications, Washington D.C., http://documents1.worldbank.org/curated/en/152581468325773312/pdf/788110NWP0Box30ucational0Resilience.pdf (accessed on 13 October 2020). [12]

UNESCO (2020), *Global monitoring of school closures caused by COVID-19*, https://en.unesco.org/covid19/educationresponse (accessed on 13 October 2020). [1]

Ungar, M. (2011), *Community resilience for youth and families: Facilitative physical and social capital in contexts of adversity*, Elsevier, Amsterdam, http://dx.doi.org/10.1016/j.childyouth.2011.04.027. [11]

1. Education actors should nurture resilient mind-sets that value people and processes over classrooms and devices

About this lesson: The COVID-19 pandemic has shaken long-accepted beliefs about education, reinforcing the notion that effective learning is determined more by people and processes than it is by physical spaces or instruments. As a moment of widespread innovation and improvisation, the current period offers an opportunity to build greater flexibility and resilience into the fundamental organising principles of our education systems. This lesson explores how governments are capitalising on this opportunity, harnessing new ways of organising teaching and learning to make education more responsive to the needs of all students, and in all contexts.

In Brief

After the Great Lockdown started in March 2020, in September, at school level, the large majority of education systems analysed had returned to on-site learning, with or without constraints on the organisation of teaching and learning. At post-secondary level, approaches adopted favoured hybrid modes of delivery. Education systems' guidance to adapt pedagogical practices for that specific academic period indicates a focus on ensuring that all learners can engage in, and benefit from, learning, followed by building capacity for change across the system, embracing personalised and flexible approaches to learning, and developing partnerships beyond education institutions. These findings inform three policy pointers for action, which aim to support policy makers to make the most of the changes brought about by the pandemic, by shifting educational practices towards greater responsiveness and resilience.

Infographic 1.1. Lesson 1 and policy pointers for action

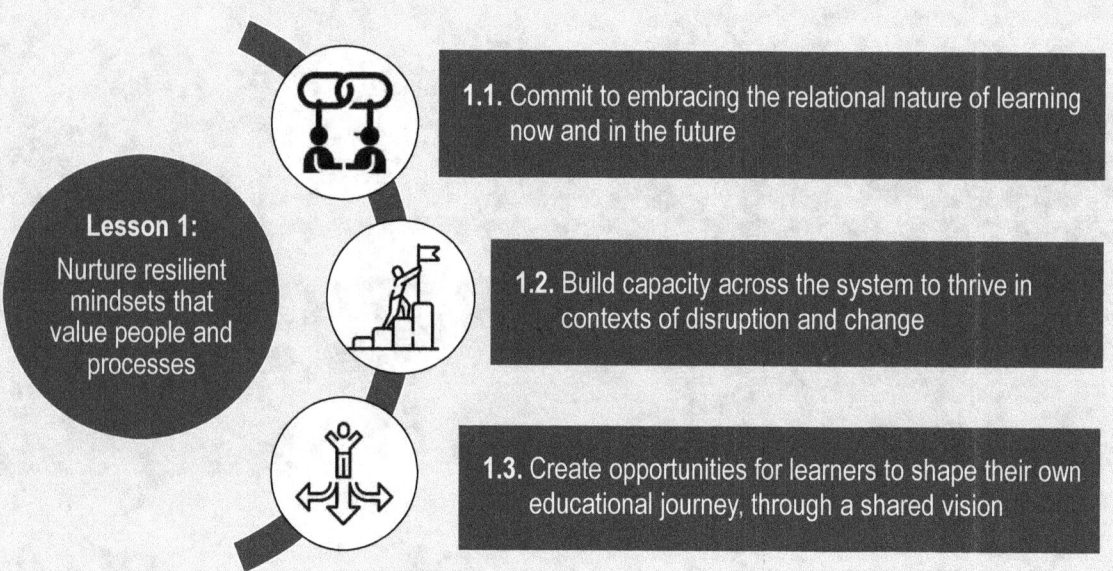

Associated resources for policy makers

▶ Annex 1. Links to government sources on delivery methods in the second half of 2020;

▶ Annex 2. Links to governments' main system-level guidelines for the second half of 2020

▶ Annex 3. Mapping of elements from governments' system-level guidelines according to the EPO's Framework for Responsiveness and Resilience in education (in process)

▶ Annex 4. Recent work from the OECD's Future of Education and Skills 2030 project in the context of the COVID-19 pandemic;

▶ Annex 5. Recent work from the OECD's Implementing Education Policies project in the context of the COVID-19 pandemic.

Background: Why now?

The crisis presents education actors with an important opportunity for change

With the COVID-19 outbreak in 2020, people, governments and economies around the world suddenly were met with a new normal. The old normal is not coming back; the looming economic crisis and current state of limbo as the world awaits a vaccine guarantee that. Before yearning for it, we should keep in mind that the often bureaucratic, hierarchical and standardised education systems of the old normal were not successfully meeting the needs of all learners in the 21st century. The priority for all those who play a role in education around the world today is hence not merely to re-establish the status quo, but to adopt a mind-set of flexibility and change, identifying and supporting approaches, both old and new, that can strengthen education and training. The insights countries have gained while handling the COVID-19 crisis therefore offer crucial foundations on which to build a new normal.

Firstly, the crisis has drawn increased attention to the notion that learning is relational and social, and not transactional. As governments ordered institutional closures, the implementation of emergency education reminded us more than ever that learning can occur anywhere and at any time. At the height of national lockdowns, countries mobilised alternative modes of teaching and learning on a massive scale: distance learning via the Internet, television, radio and even postal networks. Now, even as institutions reopen, traditional in-person approaches combine with online and other distance methods in new hybrid models. The crisis has therefore forced new flexibility into the two basic organising, as well as constraining, constructs of modern education systems: time and space (Fullan et al., 2020[1]). It reminds us that effective learning is more about relationships and mind-sets than it is about physical spaces or instruments. Moving forward, identifying how effective student learning processes and interactions can take place in contexts of disruption, as well as nurturing them with the right support systems, is a key priority for governments.

Secondly, the emergency response proved that education systems are not too heavy to move. Certainly, education reform is difficult; the unique scale and reach of the sector entails that competing opinions and vested interests often impede or divert policy implementation. Furthermore, the very nature of education generally results in a substantial lag between the time at which the initial cost of reform is incurred and that at which intended benefits materialise (or not) (Schleicher, 2018[2]). During the early stages of the pandemic, however, students, educators and administrators found themselves adapting to a completely new way of organising teaching and learning- in some cases overnight- and the world learned that big changes can happen quickly, even in education. As education systems continue to navigate uncharted waters in the second half of 2020, anyone with a stake in education delivery must hold this new truth in view: education can be more, education can be different, education can be better.

Finally, this deep global disruption emphasises the need for greater resilience. Having exposed the frailties of the complex systems of the 21st century and their single-minded pursuit of efficiency, the current crisis has brought resilience and preparedness to the forefront of public consciousness (OECD, 2020[3]). This amplifies ongoing disruption caused by other more localised crises that have affected countries to varying degrees in recent years, alongside the threat of disruption posed by an increasingly volatile global context. Only resilient education systems that plan for disruption, and withstand and recover from adverse events, will be able to fulfil the fundamental human right to education, whatever the circumstances, and foster the level of human capital required by successful economies. At the same time, resilient education systems develop resilient individuals who adjust to everyday challenges, play an active role in their communities, and respond to an increasingly volatile, uncertain and ambiguous global landscape (Schleicher, 2019[4]).With these three new insights in mind, policy makers can begin shaping policy responses that simultaneously address the needs of the new normal while shifting education practices towards a better normal. To support this process of nurturing new resilient mind-sets, the next section analyses the current state of play in 44 participating education systems across schools, vocational education and training (VET) settings and higher education institutions.

Evidence

Along with other contextual differences, the varied extent to which the COVID-19 pandemic is currently affecting countries shapes education responses in different ways. Nevertheless, some similarities have emerged and education actors can benefit from a comparative overview of the common challenges faced by their peers and the solutions being mobilised. This section explores how well-positioned education systems were prior to the crisis to strengthen learning through promoting people and processes, and identifies trends in the organisation of the current academic period in terms of the *physical delivery of education services* and the *adaptation of pedagogical practices*. Building on ongoing work by the Education Policy Outlook, it provides insights into how the guidance produced by governments in the second half of 2020 is helping to shift practices towards greater responsiveness and resilience in education.

How well placed are education systems to shift practices towards a better normal?

Education actors need to move towards a new mind-set that embraces the relational nature of learning beyond the four walls of an educational institution, but also beyond the screens of online classes. International data from the pre-crisis period can help policy makers identify system strengths and potential challenges to move towards this goal (see Figure 1.1). For example, data from the OECD's Programme for International Student Assessment (PISA) 2018 shows that the vast majority (89%) of students have both a computer for school work and internet connection at home, but a much lower share of principals (65%) report that their teachers have the technical and pedagogical skills required to effectively integrate digital devices in instruction. Similarly, on average, less than two-thirds of students across the OECD (63%) showed a growth mind-set (i.e. these students disagreed or strongly disagreed that "your intelligence is something about you that you can't change very much"), which is increasingly appearing critical for more autonomous approaches to learning. Across the OECD, socio-economically disadvantaged learners and schools performed lower for each of these indicators.

Another imbalance is that although there appears to be a strong openness to change at the level of education institutions, the conditions that allow this change to become a reality do not always exist. Some 85% of principals across the OECD consider that their schools readily accept new ideas, yet only 42% report that their staff have a significant level of responsibility in school policy, curriculum and instruction. Finally, Figure 1.1 also indicates that, prior to the crisis, there was untapped potential to strengthen synergies between the different settings in which students learn: students' learning in the workplace and relationships with parents were underdeveloped, as was system-level monitoring of school performance.

Such imbalances will need to be addressed. Successfully shifting practices in education requires a level of collective momentum only achieved when every component of the policy eco-system is working in the same direction. In the emergency conditions imposed by the COVID-19 crisis, such initial direction was clear: protect the health of learners, education providers and their families while ensuring at least a minimum level of continued education and care. Looking to the recovery phase, however, competing needs between actors make tensions more likely to arise, while governments also need to set priorities for the short and longer term, balancing the urgent and the important. Efforts to ensure alignment across the education policy eco-system may therefore require more conscious steering from the centre. These challenges were also highlighted by participants in the *Education Policy Reform Dialogues 2020*. Delegates agreed that the COVID-19 crisis had accelerated both thinking and action in education, substantially shifting attitudes within education systems in key areas of longer-term change- such as digitalisation and assessment- where there had previously been a certain level of resistance. They outlined that the challenge would be to maintain this sense of responsiveness and change in normal times as a key feature of resilience. To this end, participants noted the role of policy makers in ensuring that appropriate system-level mechanisms and means of co-ordination, steering and alignment are in place to enable local action to flourish.

Figure 1.1. Readiness for ubiquitous learning varies within and between OECD education systems

Selected indicators from the pre-crisis period (2018)

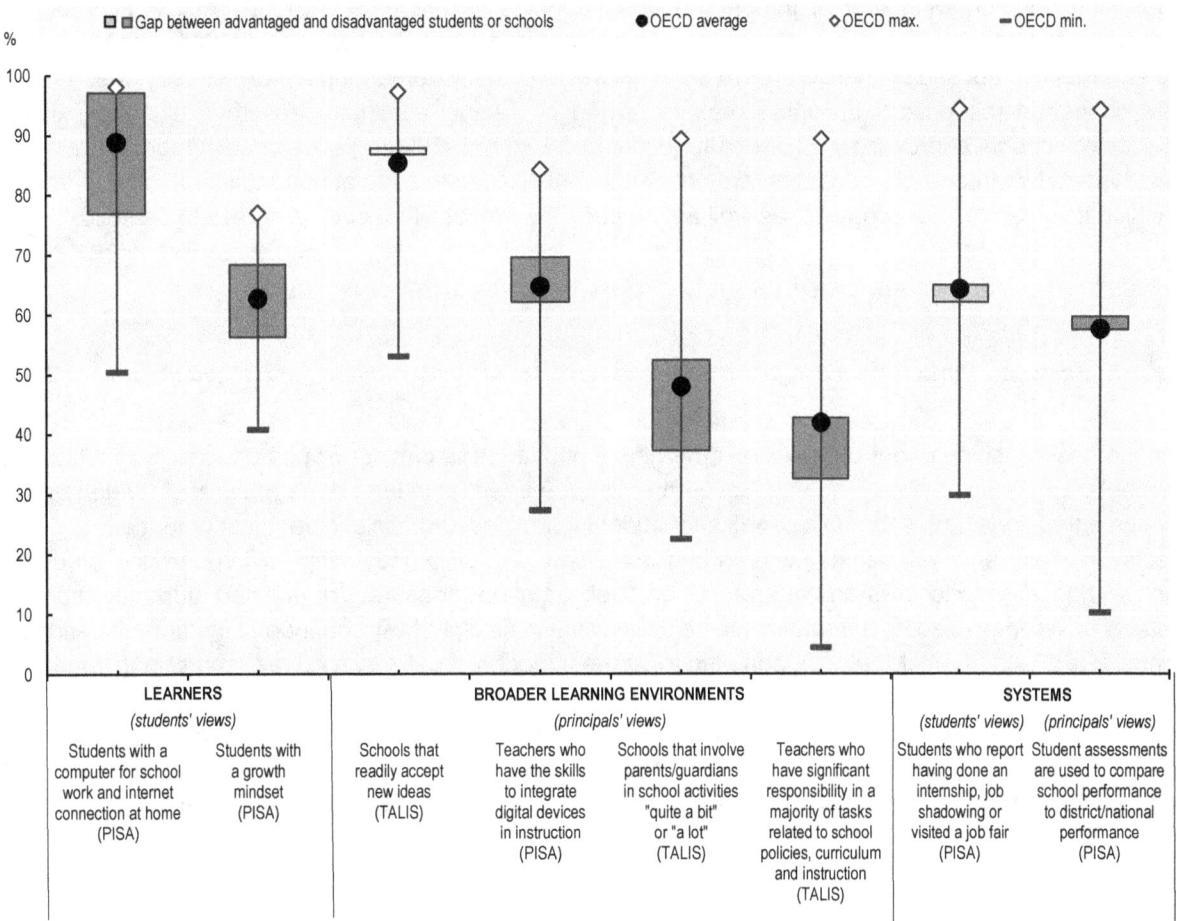

Note: Statistically significant values are shown in darker tones. The gaps between advantaged and disadvantaged schools are in blue (higher share for advantaged schools) and yellow (higher share for disadvantaged schools). Data from PISA referring to advantaged schools or students relates to those in the top quarter of the PISA index of economic, social and cultural status (ESCS); values for disadvantaged schools or students relate to those in the bottom quarter. Data from TALIS referring to advantaged schools relates to schools with a low concentration (less than or equal to 30%) of students from socio-economically disadvantaged homes; values for disadvantaged schools relates to schools with a high concentration (more than or equal to 30%) of students from socio-economically disadvantaged homes.

Source: OECD (2020[5]), *OECD Child Well-being Database*, Education and School life indicators, http://www.oecd.org/els/family/child-well-being/data/; OECD (2019[6]), *PISA 2018 database*, Table III.B1.14.3, Table V.B1.5.15/16, Table II.B1.6.11, Table V.B1.8.2, https://www.oecd.org/pisa/data/2018database/; OECD (2019[7]), *TALIS 2018 database*, Table I.2.42, Table II.5.24, Table II.5.31, https://www.oecd.org/education/talis/talis-2018-data.htm (accessed 19 November 2020).

The key components of policy eco-systems that must be aligned include core policy priorities, the existing context of the system, and key actors and the systemic arrangements required to make policies feasible and effective (OECD, 2018[8]). Policy priorities reflect the main challenges a system faces: wider structural factors such as demographic or economic developments, and system goals for the short, mid and long term. The existing context includes both the political structure and the social, cultural, and economic environments within which the education system operates. Key actors may be both decision makers and implementers, whose efforts are mediated through multi-directional interactions across central, regional and local levels. All these actors need to be engaged effectively in policy processes, fostering a sense of ownership and willingness to change, as well as the capacity to make that change happen (OECD, 2015[9]).

Finally, for policy implementation to be successful, policy makers must ensure institutional alignment with a shared long-term vision and well-planned policy monitoring or evaluation processes that can provide insight into the factors that favour or hinder successful reform implementation (OECD, 2018[8])

In normal times, achieving such alignment requires a considerable time investment in building consensus around priorities and vision, shaping a conducive context and organising wide stakeholder engagement. The emergency imposed by the COVID-19 crisis, however, initially demanded a more speedy, and indeed, more concerted response, with policy makers relying on readily available resources and the existing capacity of schools and their staff (Gouëdard, Pont and Viennet, 2020[10]). The current moment requires something between the two: education systems must mobilise knowledge at hand to identify the strengths on which they can rely for progress, as well as the gaps they must fill for such progress to be solid.

How are education systems physically organising the current academic year?

> ▶ See: Annex 1. Links to government sources on delivery methods in the second half of 2020.

As countries transitioned out of the initial emergency phase, strategies to reopen educational institutions have entailed a difficult balancing act. Governments have been facing the need to carefully weigh up the obvious educational and economic benefits to students, families and societies against potentially adverse effects on health and well-being (Reimers and Schleicher, 2020[11]). Reducing mixing between students, along with localised closures and quarantine and self-isolation measures for infected students and their contacts have been used as alternatives to help to minimise risks, but will continue to disrupt education for months (OECD, 2020[12]). Moreover, adapting to different modes of delivery requires rebalancing education resources, as well as ensuring that home environments are conducive to learning, and that teaching staff can effectively deliver instruction, whatever the learning environment. Moving forward, it is therefore essential that policy makers nurture new mind-sets that promote effective learning by valuing people and processes over physical spaces and devices. Such mind-sets will help learners and educators to transition flexibly between delivery models as required. But to what extent is this already happening?

In August and September 2020, the Education Policy Outlook conducted desk-based research to identify the current state of play in primary, secondary and post-secondary education among participating countries. Taking place six months after the COVID-19 virus was declared a global pandemic, this offers an insight into governments' priorities for education as systems move out of the initial emergency education response. Therefore, although the rapidly evolving context means delivery models continue to change, the following analysis offers an indication of possible future directions and changing mind-sets in education.

In most school systems analysed, national governments established a single, favoured approach to educational delivery for September 2020, whether that be fully remote, fully on-site or hybrid (see Figure 1.2). Such decisions took the form of an official legislative order, a formal recommendation, or guidelines for institutions and local authorities. Within this, most countries allowed for alternative measures at regional, municipal or institutional level, in accordance with the evolution of the virus. In **Austria**, a regional corona traffic light system was put in place to outline contingency measures for schools according to infection levels in the local area. In **Scotland** (United Kingdom), all young people had returned to school full-time in line with national guidance on safe reopening. However, local authorities and schools became in charge of responding to local incidents and outbreaks following local health advice and guidance; this approach saw a small number of schools close temporarily, be it on a precautionary basis or due to self-isolation requirements.

The majority of education systems analysed returned schools to a system of *on-site delivery with no constraints specific to the organisation of teaching and learning*. In these cases, although students and staff returning to school campuses followed new health and safety measures, these did not require, at least formally, significant adaptations to the organisation of teaching and learning. Such measures might include wearing a mask for teachers and some students, social distancing in non-classroom environments, and stricter cleaning regulations. In **France**, it became mandatory for staff and students in secondary education to wear masks and for schools to follow protocols regarding hand hygiene, cleaning and ventilation. Wherever possible, regulations specified that indoor spaces must be organised to allow one metre between individuals. In all these education systems, distance learning could possibly be delivered to a minority of students in self-isolation or in quarantine, and, in some countries, relaxed attendance requirements aimed to allow parents to decide whether to send children back to school or not. For example, as of 01 September 2020, with the whole of **New Zealand** on alert level two, schools had to provide on-site learning, as well as distance provisions for those self-isolating, waiting for a test result or choosing to remain at home because they are vulnerable to illness.

Another large group of education systems could allow students to remain *on-site with constraints specific to the organisation of teaching and learning*. This included limiting interactions between students by establishing contact bubbles, which might require splitting normal class sizes, reducing or modifying curricula, or adjusting timetables. For example, in **Wales** (United Kingdom), schools were advised to reduce contact between learners where possible, and many schools started operating individual class bubbles so that students in one class would not associate with those in another.

Figure 1.2. Delivery methods for the second half of 2020 (primary and secondary education)

Fully remote	Hybrid, mainly virtual	Hybrid, balanced	Hybrid, mainly on-site	On-site, with constraints specific to the organisation of teaching and learning	On-site, no constraints specific to the organisation of teaching and learning
Chile, Costa Rica, Mexico **3 countries**	Brazil², Colombia, Israel*, Kazakhstan, Turkey **5 countries**	Latvia*, Korea* **2 countries**	Canada¹ **1 country**	Canada¹, Denmark, Germany, Greece, Hungary*, Israel*, Italy, Korea*, Latvia*, Lithuania, Spain*, United Kingdom (NIRL, WLS) **13 countries**	Australia, Austria, Belgium (Fl., Fr., De.), Czech Republic, Estonia, Finland, France, Hungary*, Iceland, Ireland, Israel*, Japan, Luxembourg, Netherlands, New Zealand, Norway, Poland, Portugal, Slovak Republic, Slovenia, Spain*, Sweden, United Kingdom (ENG, SCT) **24 countries**

Notes: This table reflects desk-based research conducted by the Education Policy Outlook in August and September 2020. Due to rapidly changing contexts, some delivery methods may change during the course of 2020. Delivery methods have been categorised through analytical coding according to a best-fit approach; within every education system there is some variation. (*) Education systems that appear in more than one column have multiple approaches in place. (1) In Canada, education is the exclusive jurisdiction of the provinces and the territories. There is variation in the approaches between provinces and territories, based on their particular situations and the current impact of COVID-19 in communities. (2) In Brazil, there is variation in approaches between states (secondary education) and municipalities (primary education).
Source: See Annex 1 for a full list of the sources consulted, by education system.

In addition, there were some examples of *hybrid approaches*, with adaptations depending on the education level taught or the evolution of the virus at subnational level. In **Israel** and **Turkey**, the youngest primary level students were prioritised for on-site learning, while hybrid or fully remote solutions remained in place for older students. In **Canada**, there was variation across provinces and territories, as well as across grades in some cases, in terms of how teaching and learning were conducted. Many provinces and territories implemented a full return to in-person classes; in others, hybrid approaches were implemented for certain grades. From August, primary and secondary schools in **Korea** offered both on- and offline classes; provincial offices of education and schools have the autonomy to decide on the balance while adhering to the government's social distancing measures and guidelines. Similarly, in **Latvia**, most schools welcomed students back on site, but those schools unable to adhere to the bubble system may have had to deliver part of the curriculum online. Around one-fifth of schools, mostly upper secondary, do so. In **Brazil**, children in some federal states returned to school, but on a reduced or alternating basis, while in others, education remained virtual.

Indeed, at the other end of the spectrum, a few education systems continued to operate a *fully remote* system. These were all in Latin America, where infection levels remained high in September. These systems aimed to ensure continued education through the internet, television, radio and other remote measures. **Mexico**'s Learning at Home initiative was put in place to provide pedagogical continuity for 25 million students from preschool, primary and secondary education despite unequal internet access, by mobilising televisual and radio programming (Florencia Ripani and Zuchetti, 2020[13]).

Figure 1.3. Delivery methods for the second half of 2020 (post-secondary education)

Fully remote	Hybrid, mainly virtual	Hybrid, balanced	Hybrid, mainly on-site	On-site, with constraints specific to the organisation of teaching and learning	On-site, no constraints specific to the organisation of teaching and learning
0 countries	Brazil, Colombia, Finland, Germany, Kazakhstan, Korea **6 countries**	Austria, Ireland, Japan, Netherlands, Turkey **5 countries**	Australia, Belgium (Fl., Fr., De), Estonia, Latvia, Lithuania, New Zealand, Slovenia, Spain, Sweden, United Kingdom (ENG, NIRL, SCT, WLS) **13 countries**	Czech Republic, Hungary, Portugal **3 countries**	Denmark, France, Iceland, Norway, Poland **5 countries**

Notes: The information in this table reflects desk-based research conducted by the Education Policy Outlook in August and September 2020. Due to rapidly changing contexts, some delivery methods may change during the course of 2020. Delivery methods have been categorised through analytical coding according to a best-fit approach; within every education system there is some variation. Where identifiable, the information in this figure represents the preferred mode of delivery put forward by the government, and, where there is a difference between recommendations for domestic and international students, the information refers to domestic students specifically.
Source: See Annex 1 for a full list of the sources consulted, by education system.

When comparing approaches that governments followed by educational level in September, analysis showed that these often differed between the school level and the post-secondary level. At post-secondary level, approaches varied more substantially between and within education systems (Figure 1.3). Higher education institutions (HEIs) in OECD countries generally have full or substantial autonomy. As such, although governmental advice or guidelines regarding education delivery from September 2020 were generally in place, the final decision rested in the hands of individual institutions. Furthermore, institutions cater for a range of students and might have different delivery models in place for domestic and international students, for example.

Unlike in school education in September, most post-secondary education systems were operating a *hybrid model*, with the majority favouring in-person delivery complemented by online means where social distancing rules could not be met. For example, in **Australia**, where the national government implemented a three-step plan to ease restrictions that states and territories might implement based on their own COVID-19 conditions, each step would encourage universities and technical colleges to increase in-person delivery and prioritise hands-on, skills-based learning, wherever safe to do so.

Other education systems started operating hybrid models that appeared to lean more towards online delivery. In **Germany**, the federal states and universities focused on digital offers with on-site provision for practical and experiment-based learning, as well as introductory courses. In **Kazakhstan**, HEIs could operate under full distance learning measures or a hybrid approach. In other education systems, no single approach dominated, with considerable diversity required both between and within institutions. For example, in **Ireland,** approaches could vary across programmes according to the teaching and learning needs of various disciplines, the size of student groups, and the balance of practical and theoretical learning outcomes.

As at school level over the same period, some European education systems re-instated a fully *on-site model* for higher education, with safety measures such as masks for staff and students, social distancing measures across campus, and stricter cleaning regulations. Many non-teaching activities remained off-campus or were not offered. Recommendations in **Portugal** emphasised that in-person teaching and assessment should remain the main method of instruction but that institutions should also experiment with innovative teaching and learning practices, in which in-person education became supported by digital technologies. **Hungary** recommended that HEIs receive all healthy students and staff on site from September onwards, with full adherence to health and safety rules such as hand hygiene and wearing masks, as well as maintaining 1.5 metres between people in indoor environments, wherever possible.

Updates in November 2020

At the moment of finalising this report, perhaps the only certainty when it comes to the delivery of education is that uncertainty prevails; the landscape across participating education systems is in an ongoing state of flux. For example, in October, **Wales** (United Kingdom) announced a two-week "firebreak lockdown" in which, following one week of school holidays, only learners in pre-primary, primary and lower secondary education would return to on-site learning, with distance provision for older students. Some countries with traffic light systems, including **Austria**, **Belgium** and **Poland**, have moved to full-distance or hybrid models of learning for secondary students as infection rates rise. **British Colombia** (Canada), has maintained on-site learning for all students but has introduced a grouping system wherein clusters of students and staff (20-30 students) will primarily interact with one another for the remainder of 2020.

At *post-secondary level*, many governments have been forced to commit to more substantial changes in approach. In October, **France** announced that all higher institutions must switch to fully remote instruction, with exceptions for essential practical training only, and then only at half the usual student capacity. In **Poland**, higher education institutions also switched to fully remote instruction, except for planned classes for the final year of study and for essential practical training. In **Iceland**, universities have adopted a bubble system, where a maximum of 10 students maintain contact only with those within their assigned group. Overall, then, in contrast to the wholesale lockdowns of the first wave, governments appear to be responding to rising infection levels in light of both new scientific knowledge of the virus and its impact on children and young people, and new educational knowledge of the capacities and limits of technology and the impact of institutional closures on students and their families.

Some reflections on common challenges ahead

In terms of the physical delivery of education in September, education systems do appear to have been making use of various delivery methods for the second half of 2020. This became particularly evident at post-secondary level. Moreover, many education systems recognised that one size does not fit all; students of different ages, living in different places and studying different programmes have different needs, and these needs will change depending on the infection rate in their local community. Ultimately, while national-level guidance is important, local and institutional responsiveness are key, and most education systems- especially at post-secondary level- encourage institutions to adapt regulations, recommendations and guidelines to suit their own contexts.

However, this can lead to inconsistencies in provision, causing further challenges for policy makers. The traffic light systems mentioned above, which establish a systematic framework to be applied to all future scenarios are thus helpful in establishing some consistency and clarity. They can also help reduce the decision-making burden placed on local actors. Nevertheless, such adaptive approaches demand the active support of all stakeholders – local administrators, educators, students and parents – who must be prepared to adjust their routines, perhaps and often with little notice. This requires strong stakeholder relationships built on trust, clear communication and transparency. Such relationships are not built overnight, but stakeholder and expert consultation to support decision making can help (Gouëdard, Pont and Viennet, 2020[10]).

Ultimately, measures that showed greater openness to promoting people and processes over places and devices remained reactive; decisions were made according to the trajectory of the virus. In a better normal, such decisions will need to draw from knowledge about the pedagogical value of each mode of delivery, as well as efforts to strengthen the engagement and effective capacity of education actors to make it happen. This requires co-ordinated efforts now, at national and international level, to collect evidence about what works, when and for whom. Furthermore, as countries work to move forward into a better normal, they also need to remain open to adopting approaches that go beyond a binary delivery of education: online or in-person. A much wider spectrum of teaching and learning modes will need to play an increasingly central role in the repertoire of education systems. This includes work-based learning, community-based approaches and non-formal learning, among others. To this end, it is important to have a clear understanding of the resource constraints and possibilities facing the relevant actors for each mode of delivery (Gouëdard, Pont and Viennet, 2020[10]).

Similar challenges were raised and discussed at the *Education Policy Reform Dialogues 2020*. Delegates noted that local capacity and initiative is key for education resilience. Policy makers therefore play a critical role in ensuring that appropriate system mechanisms are in place to enable local action to flourish, but also that means of system-level co-ordination, steering and alignment are effective enough to facilitate consistency. Delegates suggested that having government officials listen and learn from key stakeholders could help to ensure that this steering is effective. They also emphasised that consistent and transparent information sharing with all stakeholders is crucial when enhancing flexibility, enabling people to support that flexibility but also to make full use of it. Furthermore, in respect to higher education in particular, although it was noted that there is now a greater will for or acceptance of digital education among education actors, delegates emphasised that rethinking and redesigning the instruction model takes time and resources.

How are education systems adapting pedagogical practices for the new normal?

> ▶ See Annex 2. Links to governments' main system-level guidelines for the second half of 2020

As the previous section shows, some hybrid modes of delivery appear to be here to stay, at least for the short term, but these models of education do not guarantee improved student learning. Indeed, evidence suggests that technology-based initiatives are more likely to reinforce existing pedagogical approaches, rather than reframe them (OECD, 2020[14]). Policy makers will therefore need to shift educational practices in key policy areas that go beyond the delivery of learning in order to stimulate wider, long-lasting change.

In this way, flexible approaches to teaching and learning can move from being an emergency response to the crisis to being at the heart of a reimagined system.

To what extent are education systems already working to shift educational practices, and what policy levers for change emerge? Through analysis of the system-level guidelines in place in 43 education systems from primary to post-secondary levels, 4 key areas of policy responses can be identified as driving education forwards in the recovery period (Figure 1.4). These areas are also relevant to the current work of the Education Policy Outlook on responsiveness and resilience in education (see Introduction and Annex 3).

Figure 1.4. Adapting pedagogical practices for the academic term of the second half of 2020

Mapping according to the main guidelines produced by ministries for education delivery at primary and post-secondary levels

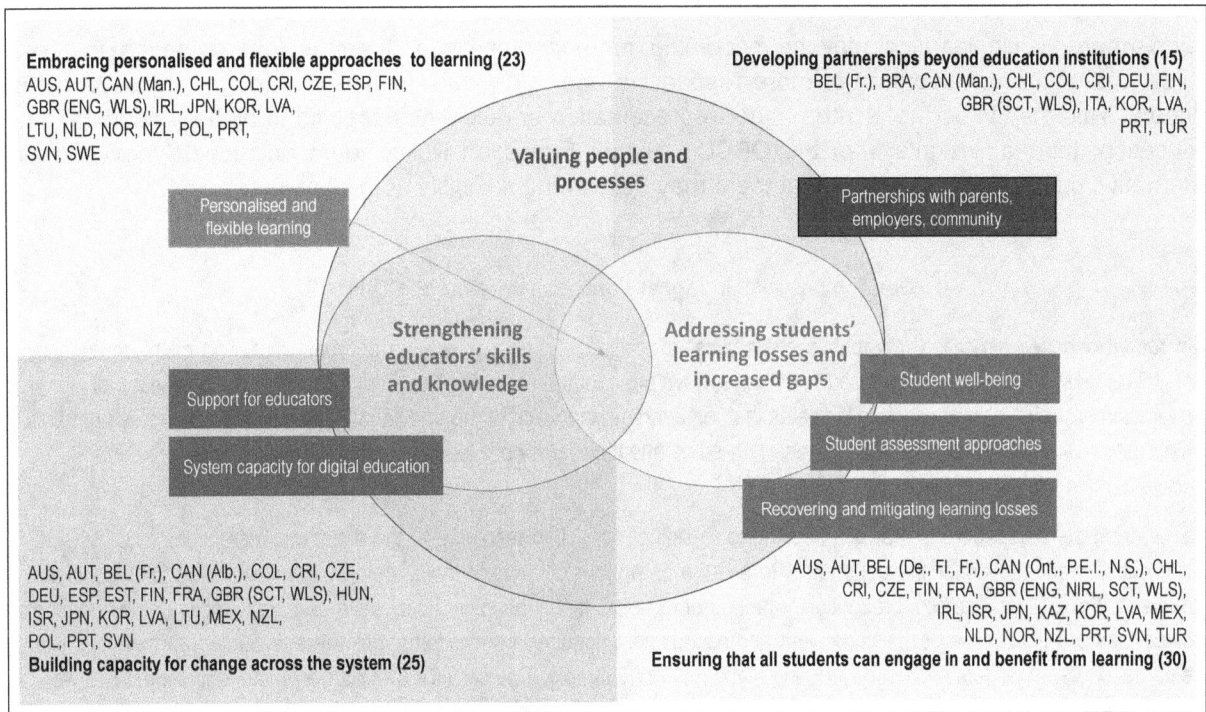

Note: The information in this figure is based on desk-based research conducted by the Education Policy Outlook between August and September 2020. The analysis captures the measures promoted by education systems through system-level guidelines, largely published between June and September 2020; other measures not reflected in this mapping may also have been implemented. In Canada, education is the exclusive jurisdiction of the provinces and the territories. There is variation in the approaches between provinces and territories. For this analysis, five of the provinces and territories were considered.
Source: See Annex 2 for a full list of the sources consulted, by education system.

Firstly, governments appear to have been *embracing more personalised and flexible approaches to learning.* In their guidelines put in place in September 2020, most education systems promote multiple delivery methods, predominantly in-person or online. To encourage greater flexibility, others have been adjusting regulatory structures, such as curriculum hours or academic calendars, or adapting curriculum planning at system, institution or teacher level. This generally involves prioritisation processes to help students achieve essential outcomes. Some guidelines analysed explicitly promote personalised learning plans, mostly for students with specific needs, and a few include guidance related to developing students' capacity for autonomous learning. In their guidelines, a smaller number of countries encourage educators to adopt cross-curricular, thematic or project-based approaches to continue exposing students to a range of subjects despite time constraints. **Slovenia** recommended that school teachers develop individual learning plans for any students who have major knowledge gaps and then create flexible learning environments that allow for group or individual implementation of these plans and for students to have some autonomy over what and when they will learn. **Korea** introduced an intensive learning system in vocational education to allow students to organise their own academic timetable, helping them to complete courses in a shorter timeframe, with theoretical elements online and practical elements in person.

However, in all these guidelines, it is less clear how accountability and capacity-building measures will be applied to help ensure quality and consistency across institutions, and how educators are being supported at the institutional level to manage the extra demands that flexibility and personalisation place on them. Prior to the crisis, less than half (47%) of lower-secondary teachers across the OECD engaged in professional development activities related to individualised learning in the 12 months prior to the OECD's Teaching and Learning International Survey (TALIS) 2018. In addition, this, along with teaching students with special educational needs and multilingual or multicultural groups of learners, was among the top five priorities for professional learning, as reported by teachers (OECD, 2019[15]).

Furthermore, while learning may be becoming more personalised, there is less evidence in these guidelines of the development of more responsive and permeable pathways through and beyond the system. This may in part reflect the under-representation of guidelines specific to higher and vocational education. Indeed, insights from the OECD's Higher Education Policy team on recent innovations in alternative credentialing suggests that there may be growing flexibility at this level (see Box 1).

Box 1. Innovation in Higher Education affected by COVID-19

In recent decades, so-called "alternative credentials" to traditional higher education degrees, including micro-credentials, digital badges, and industry-recognised certificates, have been touted as having the potential to alter the landscape of higher education provision. While evidence indicates that, on average, the value of the traditional higher education degrees remains high, alternative credentials have been receiving more attention from both learners and higher education providers in the context of the COVID-19 pandemic.

Seen from the perspective of learners seeking to re-skill or up-skill in response to the economic disruptions of COVID-19, alternative credentials offer the opportunity to acquire or signal skills that is more rapid and work-focused than traditional degrees. For HEIs, these new credentials enable them to offer highly adaptive, innovative and cost-efficient study options, since they are often based upon curriculum and assessment acquired from external providers, including partnerships with external course providers and online learning platforms. For example, *Coursera for Campus*, a partnership scheme between the online learning platform and HEIs, created more than 3 700 partnerships since its launch at the end of 2019. This type of collaboration between HEIs and educational technology companies provides them with a capacity to rapidly respond to learner demands, and may persist beyond the end of the pandemic and form part of the "new normal".

Governments, too, view shorter learning programmes as a tool to quickly up-skill and re-skill laid-off workers, and better align their skills profiles to labour market demand. For example, the Portuguese government launched the "Skills 4 post-Covid" initiative in May 2020, aiming to equip the unemployed with specialised-skills that are highly in demand in the labour market through the provision of micro-credential programmes.

> Though promising, many questions remain about these alternative credentials. There is uncertainty among quality assurance bodies and government funders about how new credentials can be incorporated into qualification frameworks, how their quality can be assured, how to fund their provision and uptake by higher education institutions and learners, and how to monitor their economic payoff to learners. Some governments are working towards integrating alternative credentials into their national quality assurance frameworks. For example, in 2018, the New Zealand Qualifications Authority (NZQA) developed a scheme to assess the quality of these new credentials and recognise those satisfying their quality standards, while the nation's Tertiary Education Commission began to offer funding to providers of these new credentials. Similar initiatives are underway both in North America and Europe.
>
> **Sources**: Gallagher, S. (2018[16]), *Educational Credentials Come of Age: A Survey on the Use and Value of Educational Credentials in Hiring*, Northeastern University, https://www.northeastern.edu/cfhets/wp-content/uploads/2018/12/Educational_Credentials_Come_of_Age_2018.pdf; Coursera (2020[17]), "Coursera for Campus", *Home*, website of Coursera, https://www.coursera.org/campus/ (accessed on 13 October 2020); Government of Portugal (2020[18]), "Skills 4 post-Covid initiative – Skills for the future", *Home – Communication – Announcements*, 18/052020, webpage of Government of Portugal, https://www.portugal.gov.pt/pt/gc22/comunicacao/comunicado?i=iniciativa-skills-4-pos-covid-competencias-para-o-futuro (accessed on 13 October 2020); Kato, S., Galán-Muros, V. and T. Weko (2020[19]), *The Emergence of Alternative Credentials*, OECD Publishing, Paris, https://doi.org/10.1787/b741f39e-en; NZQA (2019[20]), "Approval of micro-credentials", *Providers and Partners – Approval, Accreditation and Registration*, webpage of NZQA, https://www.nzqa.govt.nz/providers-partners/approval-accreditation-and-registration/micro-credentials/ (accessed 19 November 2020).
>
> **For more information** about the work of the Higher Education Policy Team, please visit https://www.oecd.org/education/higher-education-policy/.

Secondly, many countries have been *developing partnerships beyond education institutions.* Strong *relationships with parents, employers and the community* will help education systems bring together the different environments in which students learn to strengthen more personalised learning approaches. In their system-level guidelines, many education systems stress the importance of maintaining clear and regular communication with parents. Some provide specific ideas for facilitating this, including communications strategies and templates, along with recommended digital tools. A smaller group promote deeper collaboration, such as involving parents of younger learners in planning teaching content, holding regular conversations about student progress or consulting parents to inform decision making. **Colombia**'s guidelines promote the recently published Family-School Alliance strategy (2020), which furthers the principle of co-responsibility in education and care. This includes guidance for strengthening the relationship between families and the school, a communication strategy with key messaging, recommendations and information for families, and a website aimed at supporting families to strengthen their capacities for care and education.

Some education systems also encourage work with local partners in their guidelines, including education or youth workers in the local community, or specialist professionals who support students with specific needs. The **French Community of Belgium** invites schools to collaborate with a broad network of actors involved in extra-curricular activities, such as those working in supervised homework settings, youth centres, or other private and non-profit educational services. The government calls upon local education administrations and other public services to support this collaboration.

While it is encouraging that many guidelines promote the role of parents, education systems could offer more formalised approaches to parental engagement at institution or system level. Prior to the crisis, there were indications of a decline in parental engagement in some areas: according to principals' reports in PISA 2018, the share of parents engaging in local school governance or volunteering for physical or extra-curricular activities declined slightly between 2015 and 2018 (OECD, 2019[21]). Nevertheless, just over three-quarters of teachers participating in TALIS 2018 reported that their school provides parents with opportunities to actively participate in school decisions (OECD, 2020[22]). During the emergency period, **Latvia** used online parental surveys to gather feedback, which later informed guidance and support. Such efforts provide valuable rapid feedback loops to schools and governments that help strengthen implementation (OECD, 2020[23]). Another possibility could be to involve parents in the development of reopening or contingency plans which can strengthen the emergency preparedness of both institutions and families (Burns and Gottschalk, 2020[24]).

It would also be valuable to see more practical advice for institutions on developing partnerships with the private sector and local employers to support work-based learning in VET, facilitate transitions into employment, or collaborate with digital specialists. Governments should take decisive action to protect young people from the economic fallout of the pandemic. In the context of reduced demand, many employers will be less willing to take on new staff, and are likely to reduce staffing on a last in/first out basis. Moreover, young people are also more likely to work in jobs that are at a high risk of automation (Schoon and Mann, 2020[25]). In this context, many students, employees and job seekers will be looking to reassess their options or change paths. Ongoing work from the OECD's VET team offers further insight into key areas of action (see Box 2).

Box 2. How can education systems lay the foundations for resilient VET systems?

The COVID-19 crisis and ongoing structural changes in labour markets are increasing the need for VET systems around the world to be more resilient and adaptable. The OECD *VET Facing the Future* project assesses the future-readiness of VET systems in three key areas: 1) responsiveness to changing skill needs; 2) ability to develop transversal skills that allow graduates to adapt to changes in the labour market; and 3) flexibility to deliver training that is tailored to the needs of a diverse group of students – including adults in need of up-skilling or re-skilling.

In responsive VET systems, existing VET programmes are updated in a timely way to reflect changing needs in the labour market, and new programmes are created when there is sustained demand for them. Strong co-ordination between the VET system and the world of work allows for a better understanding of how jobs and skill needs are changing and how VET systems should react to these changes. Strong ties between VET providers and social partners also facilitate the implementation of work-based learning. Therefore, responsive VET systems are built upon strong engagement with social partners. Involving social partners in the design and delivery of VET fosters alignment with labour market needs, which supports employers in finding the skills they need and helps students in their school-to-work-transitions. As the evidence from previous economic downturns shows, the COVID-19 crisis might make it difficult for employers to provide work-based learning opportunities for VET students. Ensuring that employers remain engaged in VET systems will be crucial in providing students with high-quality VET programmes and avoiding skill shortages in the coming years.

Several countries have put in place financial support for employers –and especially small and medium-sized enterprises- to continue to provide work-based learning opportunities for VET students. This is the case, for example, in Australia, where a wage subsidy scheme was put in place to support ongoing and new apprenticeships. The wage subsidy scheme is part of a broader JobTrainer package that aims to provide hundreds of thousands of Australians access to new skills by retraining and up-skilling them into sectors with job opportunities as the economy recovers from COVID-19. The package also includes a JobTrainer Fund that will support the creation of additional short and long courses for school leavers and job seekers. In the context of the setup of this fund, states and territories have signed up to a new *Heads of Agreement for Skills Reform*, which sets immediate and longer-term reforms to improve the VET sector.

Sources: OECD (2020[26]), *OECD Employment Outlook 2020: Worker Security and the COVID-19 Crisis*, OECD Publishing, Paris, https://doi.org/10.1787/1686c758-en; OECD (2020[27]), *VET in a time of crisis: Building foundations for resilient vocational education and training systems*, OECD Policy Responses to Coronavirus (COVID-19), https://www.oecd.org/coronavirus/en/policy-responses; OECD (2020[28]), *Teaching and learning in VET: The impact of the COVID-19 crisis on the use of digital technologies*, OECD Policy Responses to Coronavirus; Department of Education, Skills and Employment, Australia (2020[29]), "JobTrainer package announced", webpage of Government of Australia, https://www.dese.gov.au/news/jobtrainer-package-announced (accessed on 13 October 2020).

For more information about the OECD's work on VET and adult learning, please visit http://www.oecd.org/skills/vet.htm.

Building capacity for change across the system is a third clear area of policy action in the guidelines. Education systems have been seeking to develop *system capacity for digital education*. Many systems have continued to strengthen the digital tools and infrastructure available to the education sector. This has most commonly involved guidance or advice related to online education, either through the guidelines themselves or by directing educators to other sources of information, but also the provision of digital equipment. For educators, several systems have adapted or introduced online professional development opportunities, particularly in relation to strengthening digital skills. A large share of guidelines advise educators on the type of digital solutions to adopt, with some education systems facilitating this by standardising access through a single portal or conducting quality assessments to guide educators' decision making. At school level, **Germany** has recommended that state authorities conduct a screening and evaluation of existing software and digital learning materials according to uniform, research-based criteria. **Austria** developed a range of training courses to prepare teachers for the introduction of a uniform one-stop digital platform for all schools from September. Complementing this, teachers could also access a massive open online course (MOOC) covering the organisation of distance learning, the use of digital platforms, the development of digital content, and communication with parents.

In general, the guidelines indicate that many education systems aim to move beyond simply digitising and collating educational resources for educators, as was common in the emergency phase. Rather, systems now promoted the use of more sophisticated technology, including tools for synchronous learning and peer collaboration. However, a greater emphasis was placed on technical or operational elements of more flexible approaches to learning, as opposed to pedagogical; this is particularly true for vocational and higher education. At school level, at least, this was also evident in the pre-crisis period. In PISA 2018, nearly two-thirds (62%) of school principals reported that their school had a written statement about the use of digital devices in place, but less than half (46%) reported the existence of a pedagogically oriented statement. Meanwhile, only just over one-third (36%) had a specific programme in place to promote teacher collaboration on the use of digital devices (OECD, 2020[30]).

Furthermore, although all education systems have endeavoured in their guidelines to provide *support to educators*, the focus has tended to be largely limited to developing digital skills; there are fewer measures identified to develop capacities for more personalised approaches to learning or bridging learning gaps. Moreover, there appears to be insufficient guidance regarding educator well-being. This is particularly important given that, even prior to the crisis, the highest reported causes of work-related stress among lower-secondary teachers and principals were excess administrative work and changing requirements from local, municipal/regional, state or national/federal authorities, as well as, for teachers, being held responsible for student achievement and too much marking (OECD, 2020[22]). In the context of the pandemic, a small number of education systems have been recruiting auxiliary staff to lighten the extra workload, while others have made efforts to adapt the role of local or regional advisors in order to support with implementation challenges. For instance, through **Japan**'s Human Resources Bank for Supporting Schools and Children initiative, depending on the infection rate in the region, schools may be assigned support staff to help with lesson preparation, parental communications and health management. Furthermore, additional classroom support instructors can be recruited from the national pool of retired teachers, cram-school teachers, university students and other education-related staff. Generally, however, efforts to support educators do not seem to be developing their wider capacities for change, including their resilience. Lesson two explores this issue in more detail.

Finally, countries have made efforts to *ensure that all students can engage in and benefit from learning*. Many education systems' guidelines include advice or measures for *recovering and mitigating learning gaps*. A large number have issued guidance on diagnosing learning needs on the return to in-person education. This then informs the implementation of remedial measures, which often take the form of additional learning time through extended provision on site or supplementary online learning, specialised provision for students with specific language or educational needs, and individual coaching, mentoring or supervision. As schools reopened in **Portugal**, teachers were expected to meet students individually to discuss progress during remote education and identify learning gaps. This informed the development of individual learning portfolios that outline each student's study plan and allows for more personalised monitoring by the designated teacher.

Many education systems are engaging in a much broader collection of student information for the second half of 2020, with substantial guidance for *student assessment approaches*. This includes promoting formative assessment strategies such as student self-assessment, regular teacher feedback and assessment-focused dialogue, and learning portfolios, as well as the diagnostic approaches outlined above. There is also some guidance on approaches to assessment for digital learning, including monitoring participation, implementing regular progress checks and using specific online tools for assessing and reporting on student progress. Some countries have also considered the role of assessment in hybrid delivery models and the implications for parity, academic integrity and clarity. However, the guidance provided rarely covers best practice in the dissemination or use of data on student progress, particularly by students themselves, and institutions. At school level, **Chile** promotes student-centred conferences between teachers, parents and students, and the use of learning portfolios, but has also developed several digital assessment tools. Student Online Learning assessments have aimed to allow students to send their results in core subjects to the teacher weekly and receive feedback, and specific digital assessment tools have been put in place to enable teachers to prepare their own online assessments for certain subjects, based on the key learning objectives of the curriculum.

To develop resilience, it is also critical that, when supporting learners, education systems understand and strengthen the internal world of the student. Among the few countries whose guidelines promote *student well-being* as critical in establishing the conditions for learning, particularly in the initial return to in-person teaching, two main approaches were identified: promoting the provision of specialist professional support, and encouraging educators to plan teaching and learning with well-being in mind. **Ireland** advises schools to plan for more collaborative learning to support student interaction and engagement, as well as increasing the use of the outdoor environment to engage children in physical activity and build a sense of wellness. Nevertheless, efforts identified to understand student experiences by promoting and engaging with student voice were rare. Learners have a unique perspective on their needs and experiences and involving them in the strategic improvement of education ensures that learning continues to address their needs and aspirations, even as these evolve.

At school level at least, when comparing with documents produced in the initial stages of the crisis, the guidelines indicate a clear shift in emphasis from mitigating to addressing learning gaps, as countries moved out of the initial emergency phase. However, there is less clarity regarding concrete measures to support students in vocational and higher education. Furthermore, while there are some examples of comprehensive guidelines that aimed to synthesise well-being, assessment and remedial efforts into one coherent strategy with concrete tools for schools to use, the burden generally appeared to fall upon schools or individual teachers to develop the detail.

Some reflections on common challenges ahead

A key challenge facing policy makers is how to reconcile efforts to adapt pedagogical practices with measures to protect the well-being of educators. The pandemic has placed a heavy implementation burden on institutional actors. This in turn has required them to commit more of their time to professional learning in order to acquire new skills and new knowledge. Although this emphasis on institutional actors may allow strategies to be more tailored to local contexts, such an approach risks leaving them feeling overwhelmed and more likely to need to revert to the habits of the old normal. In recognising that new delivery modes place extra demands on institutional actors' time and capacities, education systems must offer concrete measures to minimise undue burden and to ensure that such demands make full use of their professional expertise for student learning.

Although efforts to shift pedagogical practices at school level are evident across many education systems, it is less clear how governments were supporting VET providers and HEIs to implement changes that go beyond practical or logistical elements during the crisis period. Yet, the four areas of policy action identified here (personalised and flexible approaches to learning, developing partnerships, building capacity for change and ensuring all learners benefit) are as relevant to VET and higher education as they are to school education. Indeed, given the challenges facing young people entering the labour market over the coming years, and the disruption to the end-of-cycle assessment and certification processes caused by the COVID-19 pandemic, as well as the subsequent need to re-scope these processes, students progressing to or already in higher education and VET may be among the most affected by this crisis.

At the *Education Policy Reform Dialogues 2020,* delegates raised and discussed related challenges. Reiterating the heavy and continuing impact of the COVID-19 pandemic on higher education, delegates' discussions revealed the ongoing challenge to reconcile institutional autonomy and respect for academic freedom with the need for sectoral change. As such, it was noted that education systems need to establish a better understanding of the manifold components of higher education institution eco-systems in order to better provide support from public policy. Equally, delegates highlighted the fact that higher education institutions play an important wider societal function beyond students' academic learning, calling for system-level actors to sufficiently recognise this in support efforts. Regarding the VET sector, delegates shared some solutions to key challenges, but it was noted that the many, more creative solutions being implemented at local and national level would require greater support and engagement from policy makers to gain traction. These include increasing flexibility through training breaks, modularisation, part-time learning, weekend online courses, fast-tracking licensing of providers and widening access to credentials through better recognition of prior learning. Digitised training and assessment could also be explored further.

Policy pointers

This section has explored the ways in which policy makers are working to shift educational practices towards a new and better normal in which the people and processes of learning are valued over the places and devices associated with it. Taking into account the current modes of delivery, as well as system-level guidance in key policy areas and the Education Policy Outlook's Framework for Responsiveness and Resilience, three policy pointers for future action emerge:

1. Commit to embracing the relational nature of learning now and in the future

The COVID-19 crisis has reinforced the notion that learning is a relational process that can happen anywhere and at any time. Transforming education systems for the long term requires looking beyond a binary, reactive interpretation of this insight towards a model that harnesses learning in all its guises: formal and informal, curricular and extra-curricular, institution-based, home-based, community-based and work-based.

To ensure that such approaches work for all learners and help transform educational practices for the better, policy makers need to develop a deeper understanding of the educational benefits of different delivery approaches across every education level and sector. Furthermore, systems must ensure that such an approach to learning as processes helps address long-standing equity challenges as opposed to exacerbating them. This requires moving beyond the operational or organisational elements of delivery towards examining pedagogical elements that enrich learning processes and interactions between educators and learners. These elements then need to be used to inform decision making and guidance measures that support institutional actors in embracing diversity and implementing change. This is as important for driving improvement in higher and vocational education as it is in school education.

2. Build capacity for people across the system to thrive among disruption and change

Transforming education requires shifting practices at every level of the system. This cannot happen without co-ordinated efforts to build capacity for change, supplying all actors in the system with the skills and knowledge required to implement something new. Although capacity-building efforts are in place in the second half of 2020, the focus remains largely limited to building digital skills among educators.

Building capacity for system transformation requires adopting a much broader view. Educators need support to effectively diagnose every learner's learning needs, plan appropriate and differentiated remedial action, and monitor progress towards learning goals. Parents and students also need to be empowered to participate actively in this process. Lesson two further explores how policy makers can design and implement effective policy efforts to support professional learning for educators. Institutions, their leaders, and local education administrators will need to develop the necessary skills to collaborate with people they may not be used to working with, and to lead their staff in adapting practices to local contexts, finding innovative solutions to local problems. Finally, this all begins with policy makers, whose ability to collate and disseminate evidence and knowledge about policy processes is crucial in shifting mind-sets and transforming education into something new and better.

3. Create opportunities for learners to shape their own educational journey, through a shared vision

Students should be supported in developing the skills required for more autonomous learning – self-regulation and self-evaluation, as well as digital skills – but also the skills and knowledge required to support well-being. Furthermore, only education systems that truly listen to students' needs, ambitions and lived experiences, and that act on that information, will be responsive enough to successfully engage all learners, even as individuals and societies change.

In the specific context of the second half of 2020, this starts with mitigating and recovering the learning gaps that may have appeared as a result of emergency distance education to ensure that all learners continue to progress through the system, recognising that protecting and strengthening student well-being is a crucial precursor. Viewing this crisis as a syndemic, education systems need to support learner recovery by identifying the full breadth of academic and socio-emotional needs of all learners and aligning them to more personalised learning opportunities. Many education systems considered in this report have implemented guidance and initiatives that show evidence of this; Lesson three further explores how policymakers can design and implement effective policy efforts in this area. Similarly, education systems need to increase the flexibility of their education pathways so that learners can better adapt theirs to respond to changes of context; this flexibility needs, however, to be provided through a shared vision at the system level of what it means to become a thriving learner.

Other relevant OECD work

Insights from other OECD work can also help inform policy makers' responses in the current context:

- The *Future for Education and Skills 2030* project has been working to gain clarity on what students need to learn in order to become citizens of future thriving societies, and how this new curriculum should be implemented, including in the context of the COVID-19 pandemic (See **Annex 4**).
- Similarly, the *Implementing Education Policies project* has developed a framework to help governments structure the implementation strategy of their evolving education responses to COVID-19 in schools (see **Annex 5**).

References

Burns, T. and F. Gottschalk (eds.) (2020), *Education in the Digital Age: Healthy and Happy Children*, Educational Research and Innovation, OECD Publishing, Paris, https://dx.doi.org/10.1787/1209166a-en. [24]

Coursera (2020), *Coursera for Campus*, http://dx.doi.org/www.coursera.org/campus/ (accessed on 13 October 2020). [17]

Department of Education, Skills and Employment, Australia (2020), *JobTrainer package announced*, Australian Government, Canberra, https://www.dese.gov.au/news/jobtrainer-package-announced (accessed on 13 October 2020). [29]

Florencia Ripani, M. and A. Zuchetti (2020), "Mexico: Aprende en Casa (Learning at home)", in, *Education Continuity Stories Series*, OECD Publishing, Paris, https://oecdedutoday.com/wp-content/uploads/2020/07/Mexico-Aprende-en-casa.pdf (accessed on 13 October 2020). [13]

Fullan, M. et al. (2020), *Education Reimagined; The Future of Learning*, A collaborative position paper between New Pedagogies for Deep Learning and Microsoft Education., http://aka.ms/HybridLearningPaper (accessed on 13 October 2020). [1]

Gallagher, S. (2018), *Educational Credentials Come of Age: A Survey on the Use and Value of Educational Credentials in Hiring*, Center for the Future of Higher Education and Talent Strategy, Northeastern University, Boston, http://www.northeastern.edu/cfhets/wp-content/uploads/2018/12/Educational_Credentials_Come_of_Age_2018.pdf (accessed on 13 October 2020). [16]

Gouëdard, P., B. Pont and R. Viennet (2020), "Education responses to COVID-19: Implementing a way forward", *OECD Education Working Papers*, No. 224, OECD Publishing, Paris, https://dx.doi.org/10.1787/8e95f977-en. [10]

Government of Portugal (2020), *Skills 4 post-Covid initiative - Skills for the future*, Governement of Portugal, Lisbon, http://www.portugal.gov.pt/pt/gc22/comunicacao/comunicado?i=iniciativa-skills-4-pos-covid-competencias-para-o-futuro (accessed on 13 October 2020). [18]

Kato, S., V. Galán-Muros and T. Weko (2020), "The emergence of alternative credentials", *OECD Education Working Papers*, No. 216, OECD Publishing, Paris, https://dx.doi.org/10.1787/b741f39e-en. [19]

NZQA (2019), *Approval of micro-credentials*, Government of New Zealand, https://www.nzqa.govt.nz/providers-partners/approval-accreditation-and-registration/micro-credentials/ (accessed on 13 October 2020). [20]

OECD (2020), *Back to the Future of Education: Four OECD Scenarios for Schooling*, Educational Research and Innovation, OECD Publishing, Paris, https://dx.doi.org/10.1787/178ef527-en. [14]

OECD (2020), "Building back better: A sustainable, resilient recovery after COVID-19", *OECD Policy Responses to Coronavirus (COVID-19)*, OECD Publications, Paris, https://read.oecd-ilibrary.org/view/?ref=133_133639-s08q2ridhf&title=Building-back-better-_A-sustainable-resilient-recovery-after-Covid-19 (accessed on 13 October 2020). [3]

OECD (2020), "Coronavirus special edition: Back to school", *Trends Shaping Education Spotlights*, No. 21, OECD Publishing, Paris, https://dx.doi.org/10.1787/339780fd-en. [12]

OECD (2020), "Education Policy Outlook: Latvia", *Education Policy Outlook Country Profiles* OECD Publishing, Paris, http://www.oecd.org/education/policy-outlook/country-profile-Latvia-2020.pdf (accessed on 13 October 2020). [23]

OECD (2020), "OECD Child Well-being", *OECD Child Well-being Portal* (database), OECD Publishing, Paris, http://www.oecd.org/els/family/child-well-being/data/ (accessed on 13 October 2020). [5]

OECD (2020), *OECD Employment Outlook 2020: Worker Security and the COVID-19 Crisis*, OECD Publishing, Paris, https://dx.doi.org/10.1787/1686c758-en. [26]

OECD (2020), *PISA 2018 Results (Volume V): Effective Policies, Successful Schools*, PISA, OECD Publishing, Paris, https://dx.doi.org/10.1787/ca768d40-en. [30]

OECD (2020), *TALIS 2018 Results (Volume II): Teachers and School Leaders as Valued Professionals*, TALIS, OECD Publishing, Paris, https://dx.doi.org/10.1787/19cf08df-en. [22]

OECD (2020), "Teaching and learning in VET: The impact of the COVID-19 crisis on the use of digital technologies", *OECD Policy Responses to Coronavirus (COVID-19)*. [28]

OECD (2020), "VET in a time of crisis: Building foundations for resilient vocational education and training systems", *OECD Policy Responses to Coronavirus (COVID-19)*, OECD Publishing, Paris, http://www.oecd.org/coronavirus/policy-responses/vet-in-a-time-of-crisis-building-foundations-for-resilient-vocational-education-and-training-systems-efff194c/ (accessed on 13 October 2020). [27]

OECD (2019), "PISA 2018", *PISA* (database), OECD Publishing, Paris, https://www.oecd.org/pisa/data/2018database/ (accessed on 13 October 2020). [6]

OECD (2019), *PISA 2018 Results (Volume III): What School Life Means for Students' Lives*, PISA, OECD Publishing, Paris, https://dx.doi.org/10.1787/acd78851-en. [21]

OECD (2019), "TALIS 2018", *TALIS (database)*, OECD Publishing, Paris, https://www.oecd.org/education/talis/talis-2018-data.htm (accessed on 13 October 2020). [7]

OECD (2019), *TALIS 2018 Results (Volume I): Teachers and School Leaders as Lifelong Learners*, TALIS, OECD Publishing, Paris, https://dx.doi.org/10.1787/1d0bc92a-en. [15]

OECD (2018), *Education Policy Outlook 2018: Putting Student Learning at the Centre*, OECD Publishing, Paris, https://dx.doi.org/10.1787/9789264301528-en. [8]

OECD (2015), *Education Policy Outlook 2015: Making Reforms Happen*, OECD Publishing, Paris, https://dx.doi.org/10.1787/9789264225442-en. [9]

Reimers, F. and A. Schleicher (2020), *Schooling Disrupted, Schooling Rethought: How the COVID-19 Pandemic is Changing Education*, OECD Publications, Paris, https://www.educatemagis.org/wp-content/uploads/documents/2020/07/document.pdf (accessed on 13 October 2020). [11]

Schleicher, A. (2019), *PISA 2018: Insights and Interpretations*, OECD Publications, Paris, https://www.oecd.org/pisa/PISA%202018%20Insights%20and%20Interpretations%20FINAL%20PDF.pdf (accessed on 13 October 2020). [4]

Schleicher, A. (2018), *World Class: How to Build a 21st-Century School System*, Strong Performers and Successful Reformers in Education, OECD Publishing, Paris, https://dx.doi.org/10.1787/9789264300002-en. [2]

Schoon, I. and A. Mann (2020), *School-to-work transitions during coronavirus: Lessons from the 2008 Global Financial Crisis*, OECD Publishing, Paris,, https://oecdedutoday.com/school-work-during-coronavirus-2008-global-financial-crisis/ (accessed on 13 October 2020). [25]

2. Educators need new skills and new knowledge to capitalise on new education priorities and means of delivery

About this lesson: During the COVID-19 pandemic, governments relied on educators to be the guarantors of children's learning, calling on them to respond innovatively in the face of great change. As new, more flexible approaches to the delivery of education look likely to outlive the pandemic, and education systems work to shift practices towards greater responsiveness and resilience, governments must prioritise professional learning and support for educators. With this in mind, this lesson explores ways in which policy makers can design and implement effective professional learning activities that simultaneously enhance educators' skills and knowledge while strengthening resilience and enabling them to thrive in changing contexts.

In Brief

Professional learning that supports educators in navigating ever-changing contexts is a central component of responsive education systems. Professional learning is also identified as a key policy lever for educator resilience, along with educator well-being, collaboration and leadership of learning. Successful policy experiences from the pre-crisis period show that professional learning which builds on the synergies between these policy levers and identified components of effective professional learning can have a positive impact on educators' confidence, their sense of being valued, their capacity for reflection and their professional relationships. More recent policy efforts in this area introduced in response to the COVID-19 pandemic show a willingness among policy makers to promote collaboration and design learning opportunities grounded in educators' everyday experiences, but also indicate a need to consider the sustainability and reach of such initiatives. These findings inform three policy pointers for action, which aim to support policy makers to develop quality professional learning opportunities that enable educators to make the most of the opportunities brought about by the pandemic and strengthen their resilience in the face of future disruption and change.

Infographic 2.1. Lesson 2 and policy pointers for action

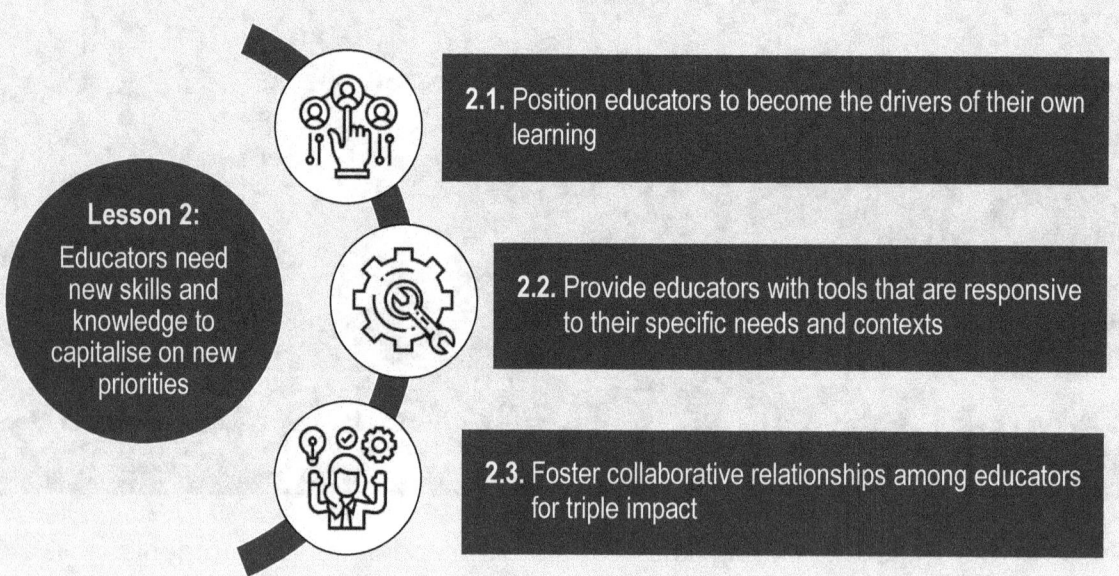

Associated resources (See Annexes)

- ▶ Annex 6. Professional learning policies from the pre-crisis period with evidence of positive impact;
- ▶ Annex 7. Selected current policy efforts to support professional learning;
- ▶ Annex 8. Recent work from the OECD's Teachers' Professional Learning Study.

Background: Why now?

The crisis emphasises an ongoing need for resilient educators

Resilient education systems require resilient educators who can react confidently to everyday challenges, and adapt positively to longer-term evolutions (Beltman, Mansfield and Price, 2011[1]; Gu and Day, 2007[2]; Kangas-Dick and O'Shaughnessy, 2020[3]) Today's educators must find innovative solutions to new and older challenges, and respond flexibly in the face of great change. Today's policy makers must therefore create the necessary conditions to ensure that at the heart of every educational institution, across all levels and sectors of the system, is a professional body of educators who are thriving and not just surviving.

Throughout the COVID-19 pandemic thus far, education systems have relied on educators to be the guarantors of children and young people's education. As schools closed across the world, teachers remained central to the delivery of alternative learning: two-thirds of respondents in a recent OECD-Harvard survey of 59 countries indicated that students were accessing the curriculum directly from their usual classroom teachers (Reimers and Schleicher, 2020[4]). This occurred predominantly online but also via telephone, radio and postal networks, demanding that educators rapidly develop new skills and knowledge.

In the second half of 2020, as education systems entered a recovery phase and many returned to full or partial on-site delivery, the role of educators changed once again. New health regulations put in place meant that educators started operating in changed environments following new routines; many started simultaneously teaching learners in the classroom and learners at home. They became more likely to be called upon to provide emotional support to students and families negatively impacted by health or economic crises, and to participate in strategic planning and decision making (OECD, 2020[5]). Often, these new tasks were placed upon educators with only the same resources as were available to them in the old normal and while trying to protect their own health and well-being.

Yet pre-crisis demands on the profession have also endured. The rapid societal and technological change of the 21st century requires educators to develop an ever broader and more complex set of skills in their students while continuously updating their own competencies (Révai, 2020[6]; Viac and Fraser, 2020[7]; Boeskens, Nusche and Yurita, 2020[8]). In parallel, increasingly diverse student bodies, more advanced technological tools and growing resource constraints in many systems have meant that, pandemic or no pandemic, educators' working environments have become increasingly challenging (OECD, 2018[9]).

These competing demands can negatively affect educators' motivation and many education systems were experiencing teacher shortages prior to the pandemic (Viac and Fraser, 2020[7]). The challenge has become particularly pronounced in higher education: a growing reliance on temporary contracts for academic staff introduced new instability, with digitalisation looking increasingly likely to transform the organisation of academic work and relationships between learners and educators (OECD, 2020[10]).

Lesson one of this handbook explored the opportunity for education systems to nurture a mind-set for learning that values people and processes over places and devices. Approaching education in this way can enhance overall resilience. However, this entails providing greater support to educators in the current context of change and building their capacity to shift to practices where learning can occur in a wider variety of forms. This requires continuing and strengthening ongoing efforts to enhance digital skills, but also providing professional learning around more personalised and flexible learning approaches, assessment practices and collaboration with a range of partners.

Lesson two also explores how policy makers can design and implement policy efforts that address these two challenges simultaneously, effectively building capacity among educators while also strengthening the resilience of the profession. What do we already know about professional learning and building educators' resilience? What related policy efforts are education systems implementing in the second half of 2020 and how can they be strengthened?

Evidence

To support the development of the skills and knowledge that can help educators better cope with current challenges, this section offers highlights of relevant international evidence about educator resilience and professional learning. Based on evidence of evaluations from policies already in place before the pandemic, it also offers insights for policy makers into policy levers and approaches that can promote resilience and responsiveness in educators, as well as some ongoing challenges. The section also looks into a selection of relevant policies implemented in the context of the COVID-19 pandemic.

What does international evidence say about professional learning and resilience?

Complementing what we already knew about keeping teachers in the role with what we have learned in 2020 about supporting teachers to thrive in a crisis, four policy levers for educator resilience emerge as part of the OECD Framework for Responsiveness and Resilience in Education, currently under development (see Introduction). **Educator well-being** (self-efficacy, job satisfaction, working conditions and relationships) directly influences motivation to either to stay in the profession or leave, while informal and formal opportunities for **collaboration** can foster personal and professional development and strengthen support mechanisms (OECD, 2020[11]; Viac and Fraser, 2020[7]). Framing all educators as **leaders of learning** by offering them a certain level of professional autonomy and capacity for innovation empowers them to become agents of change (OECD, 2020[11]). Finally, effective **professional learning** promotes continuous positive development, simultaneously strengthening both a sense of self-efficacy and actual effectiveness (Beltman, Mansfield and Price, 2011[1]; Boeskens, Nusche and Yurita, 2020[8]).

Based on these four policy levers, OECD data offers some insight into aspects of teacher resilience in the pre-crisis period (see Figure 2.1). This can serve as a useful starting point for policy makers considering how best to strengthen teacher resilience now and for the longer term. For example, while a large share of lower-secondary teachers across the OECD report engaging in impactful professional learning, there is an opportunity to strengthen certain aspects of well-being and collaboration. Teachers' views varied largely when reporting that they participated in networks of teachers specifically for their professional development, or regarding the value of the teaching profession in society. In the current context, where educators require new skills and knowledge in order to capitalise on opportunities offered by the crisis, building on the stronger areas of resilience to address weaker areas can help education systems secure quick wins. Specifically, this requires mobilising professional learning initiatives based on what we already know about successful professional learning and transforming them into opportunities to strengthen educator well-being, collaboration or leadership of learning.

Figure 2.1. Certain policy levers for educators' resilience require strengthening across the OECD

Selected indicators of educator resilience in the pre-crisis period (2018)

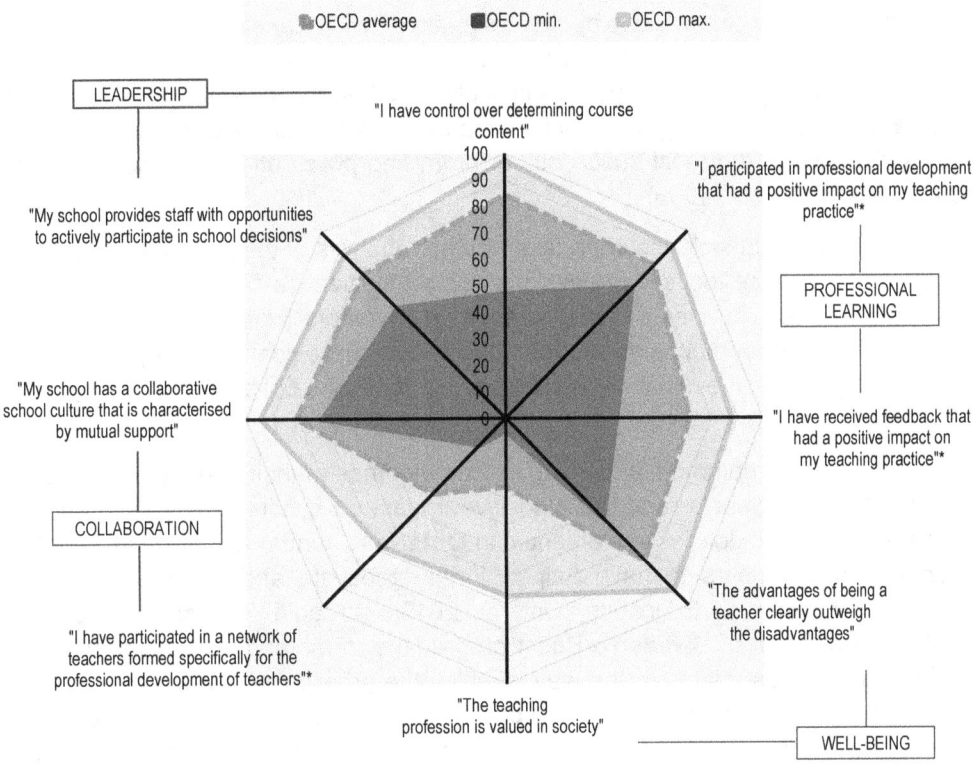

Note: Values based on the responses of lower-secondary teachers.
Source: OECD (2019[12]), *OECD TALIS 2018 Database*, Table II.5.32, Table I.5.15, Table II.4.48, Table II.2.10, Table II.2.1, Table I.5.7, Table II.4.24, Table II.4.34, https://www.oecd.org/education/talis/talis-2018-data.htm (accessed 19 November 2020).

How can educators benefit from high-quality professional learning that can effectively nurture the other levers of educator resilience? The OECD's TALIS project identifies 12 components of effective professional learning from the specialist literature (OECD, 2019[13]). These are further grouped into four key policy components:

- **Content focus**: Effective professional learning has strong subject and curriculum-based components that help teachers strengthen their classroom practice (Darling-Hammond, Hyler and Gardner, 2017[14]). It is also coherent with teachers' prior skills, knowledge and experience and their professional needs and goals.
- **Active learning and collaboration**: Active learning enables teachers to design and try out teaching strategies, generally in a classroom setting, providing a more authentic learning opportunity that is highly contextualised to their students (Darling-Hammond, Hyler and Gardner, 2017[14]). Collaborative approaches encourage participants to share ideas and co-operate on shared challenges. In this way, it incentivises the peer learning and coaching approaches deemed to be a more flexible and efficient way of providing professional learning (OECD, 2019[13]).
- **A school-embedded approach**: School-embedded professional development grounds learning in the teacher's everyday working context and is therefore more likely to shape teaching practice.
- **A sustained duration**: Although teachers usually receive professional learning as one-off activities or short programmes (e.g. courses and seminars), evidence suggests that activities with a sustained duration are more effective, affording participants the time to learn, practice, implement, and reflect upon new strategies (Darling-Hammond, Hyler and Gardner, 2017[14]; OECD, 2019[13]).

What can we learn from successful professional learning policies already in place?

While international evidence indicates key characteristics of resilience-focused professional learning initiatives, policy analysis can help illustrate how such initiatives can be planned and implemented. According to previous analysis undertaken by the Education Policy Outlook between 2008 and 2019, ensuring a cohort of high-quality teachers was the second-highest area of policy activity among participating countries, with over 80 related policies collected in 31 education systems. A further 15 policies collected by the OECD focused on supporting school leaders. Initial analysis of the progress and impact of these policies indicated that the most successful or promising policy efforts focused on collaboration, mentoring and dialogue (OECD, 2019[15]).

In 2020, the Education Policy Outlook has undertaken further analysis of these policies in order to identify successful examples of resilience-focused professional learning initiatives Table 2.1 lists the main policies selected for this analysis. These policies all aim to strengthen educators' professional skills and knowledge and also benefit from key policy components aligned with international evidence, policy levers for resilience and responsiveness, and policy evaluation outcomes that indicate positive progress towards policy objectives.

What do these policies have in common, according to the outcomes of their evaluation studies? Firstly, a recurring strength is that participants reported a positive impact on building confidence and a sense of being valued. This is the case in policies implemented in **Ontario** (Canada) and **Wales** (United Kingdom), for example. This in turn appears to have helped further motivate and engage educators in their professional practice (Ministry of Education, Ontario, 2019[16]; Arad Research and ICF Consulting, 2018[17]). Indeed, an evaluation of **Sweden**'s Boost programme in mathematics found that the positive impact on participants was less related to the way in which the programme was implemented; the most important factor started with the programme having been implemented at all. This positive impact is most apparent in professional learning policies that target specific training initiatives at specific audiences, rather than adopting a one-size-fits-all approach.

Another benefit evidenced in several evaluations was the opportunity to develop more reflective practitioners. Many of the educators involved in piloting **Ireland**'s National Professional Development Framework for Higher Education, regardless of role, specifically valued the Framework as a tool for supporting reflection. Similarly, school leaders receiving coaching through **Ireland**'s Centre for School Leadership described the positive impact of the coaching experience as "learning the discipline of reflection". Indeed, across numerous selected policies, including in **Denmark**, **Ireland** and **Ontario** (Canada) a commonly cited implementation challenge was the lack of time for educators to fully engage with the material or programme – a lack of time for reflection.

Building strong relationships was both an important part of implementing many of these policies, and a positive outcome. In the New Teacher Induction programme in **Ontario** (Canada), the opportunities created for informal mentorship or support from colleagues were seen as particularly helpful, and relationships were key in successful implementation, not just between mentors and mentees but also between the mentors themselves. **France**'s network of Digital Education Advisors were a key asset during the COVID-19 crisis because their strong relationships with all major stakeholders in the field enabled quick negotiations with partners, rapid communication and an understanding of the specificities of different local contexts.

Table 2.1. Professional learning policies from the pre-crisis period with evidence of positive impact

Education system	Education level	Policy and year	Policy levers for responsiveness and resilience	Key policy components
Ontario (Canada)	Schools	Expansion of New Teacher Induction Programme (2009)	Well-being	Content focus, Active learning & collaboration, Sustained duration
Denmark	Schools	National Corps of Learning Consultants (2014)	Collaboration	School embedded
Finland	Schools	Network of tutor-teachers for basic education (2016)	Collaboration, Leadership	Content focus, Sustained duration, School embedded
France	Schools	Network of digital education advisors (2014)	Collaboration	Content focus, Sustained duration
Ireland	Schools	Centre for School Leadership (2015)	Well-being, Leadership	Content focus, Active learning & collaboration, Sustained duration
Ireland	Higher education	National Professional Development Framework for Higher Education (2016)	Leadership	Content focus, School embedded
New Zealand	Schools	Communities of learning | *Kahui Ako* (2014)	Collaboration, Leadership	Active learning & collaboration, Sustained duration, School embedded
Norway	Schools	Advisory Team Programme (2009); Follow Up Scheme (2017)	Leadership	Sustained duration, School embedded
Portugal	Schools	Strengthening the School Association Professional Development Centres (2014)	Leadership	Content focus, School embedded
Sweden	Schools	Collaborative research-based learning projects for teachers (2012)	Collaboration, Leadership	Content focus, Active learning & collaboration, Sustained duration
Wales (United Kingdom)	Schools	Pioneer Schools Network (2015)	Well-being, Collaboration, Leadership	Content focus, Sustained duration, School embedded

Note: Recognising the wide and varied implications that policies have on education policy eco-systems, the selected policies for this table have been coded according to the key policy levers of responsiveness and resilience and key policy components of which they make direct use.
Source: For descriptions of these policies, sources and further references by country, see Annex 6.

Finally, a clear feature of these selected policies relates to addressing needs at a local level. All the selected policies have aimed to be well-aligned either to individual teachers' needs in the classroom (content focus) or to schools' needs (school-embedded). The key strength of **Portugal**'s School Association Professional Development Centres, for example, was identified as being their ability to respond to the authentic challenges faced by educators in schools in different areas across the country. However, a more localised or personalised focus also requires ensuring consistency across localities and coherence with system goals. For policies that establish new support roles for educators' professional learning, such as **Denmark**'s Learning Consultants or **Finland**'s Digital Tutor-Teachers, professionalising and standardising the practice of those in support roles, while ensuring they respond to individual needs, is also an aspect to be enhanced.

Some reflections on common challenges ahead

Challenges regarding the high diversification of the teaching profession can also be identified. Evaluations of policies implemented in **Denmark**, **Ireland** and **Sweden** for example, noted that impact was not as positive among upper secondary practitioners as among their primary counterparts. This suggests that, in view of the very different roles these educators have, rather than trying to cover teachers at all levels, it may be more impactful to design professional learning programmes with staff from a specific education level in mind. Indeed, teaching is a highly differentiated profession. In light of this, and the fact that only one policy targeting higher education was collected for this report, the higher levels of education may require more policy attention. Furthermore, as the economic impact of the COVID-19 crisis begins to materialise and resource constraints risk becoming tighter in the future, establishing ways of targeting professional learning to areas of highest need for the medium and longer term will be important.

There are further challenges related to strategic approaches in education policy: several of the policies selected here, such as those in **Norway** and **Portugal**, began as small-scale and/or operate on a voluntary basis, and have found it difficult to reach the staff most in need of professional learning. Scaling up delivery to achieve a wider reach across the education system has also been challenging, with many systems questioning the long-term sustainability and durability of these programmes. Despite this, there is a clear sense across many of these initiatives, including those in **Denmark**, **Ireland** and **New Zealand**, that the longer the programme is in place, the better. A longer duration allows the programme to be adapted and perfected in light of feedback and evaluation results.

These challenges were raised and discussed at the *Education Policy Reform Dialogues 2020*. Delegates emphasised the need to properly identify professional learning needs before developing appropriate tools and suggested developing self-assessment instruments for teachers, in digital competence for example, or working with teacher networks to undertake peer assessment of needs. Another suggested solution was to systematise efforts to detect teacher training needs by listening to teachers themselves, through a large-scale symposium, for example. In terms of scaling up delivery, delegates suggested establishing mechanisms to enable more proficient teachers to share insights with the wider community, as well as engaging in qualitative research to better identify and understand best practice.

What can we learn from efforts to strengthen professional learning during the crisis?

> ▶ See Annex 7. Selected current policy efforts to support professional learning

Professional learning has been a focus of education systems' responses to the COVID-19 crisis. In an OECD-Harvard survey, 80% of senior government officials and education administrators identified providing professional support and advice to teachers as the focus of education continuity strategies in the initial phase of disruption; among teachers and school administrators, the share was 73% (Reimers and Schleicher, 2020[4]). The most common support measure reported was providing access to resources; around 90% of respondents reported implementing such measures. This often involved the collation of digital resources online. In recent work with countries to explore initial educational responses to the COVID-19 crisis, the Education Policy Outlook identified several practices of this type. The **Czech Republic**, for example, established a website to centralise advice, guidelines and tools for educators, parents and students from primary to tertiary level, and published a set of best practices for distance learning. The Czech National Pedagogical Institute also ran regular webinars, published blogs and established a Facebook group offering technical support to educators (OECD, 2020[18]).

In the same OECD-Harvard survey, a similar share of respondents (87%) reported participation in peer networks within schools as a common support measure for educators. Participation in networks across schools was less common, with only half (50%) of school staff reporting such provision (Reimers and Schleicher, 2020[4]). However, the Education Policy Outlook's previous work has identified interesting examples of cross-school peer collaboration and collective action. To complement digital provision, **Latvia** launched Your Class, daily educational programmes broadcast on national television and online. As part of this initiative, a group of over 70 teachers from across the country developed the educational content, with support from a voluntary parents' group (OECD, 2020[19]). **Portugal** also established a brigade of over 100 educators from the regional teams of the Autonomy and Curricular Flexibility project and other pre-existing national projects to support educators in adapting teaching and collecting and disseminating best practice (OECD, 2020[20]).

As many education systems move to reopen educational institutions, measures for professional learning remains a point of focus. In the same OECD-Harvard survey, when asked about reopening plans, 63% of senior government officials and education administrators identified training for teachers as a feature, compared to 74% of teachers and school administrators. The most common measures were counselling for teachers and training for teachers or school leaders either before or after reopening schools (Reimers and Schleicher, 2020[4]).

The Education Policy Outlook conducted desk-based research to identify other promising initiatives for professional learning planned for implementation in the second half of 2020. The policies focused on building capacity among educators to support the effective reopening of institutions and reorganisation of teaching and learning. The policies also appear to have at least one of the four key policy components of effective professional learning (content focus, active learning and collaboration, sustained school-embedded approach). They address at least two policy levers for educator responsiveness and resilience, as identified by the EPO Framework for Responsiveness and Resilience in education (professional learning and well-being, collaboration and/or leadership of learning), currently under development. In total, nine policies were selected: most focused on schools, with two aimed at higher education and one specifically targeting staff in vocational institutions (see Table 2.2).

Table 2.2. Promising policy initiatives for professional learning implemented in 2020

Education system	Education level	Policy	Policy levers for responsiveness and resilience	Key policy components
Australia	VET	A new Regulatory Strategy for VET	Well-being	Active learning and collaboration, Sustained duration
Chile	Schools & VET	Online Learning for Teachers portal	Well-being	Content focus
Chile	Schools	Distance mentoring for management teams	Leadership	Active learning and collaboration, School embedded
Colombia	Schools	Adaptation of the Let's All Learn programme	Well-being	Content focus
France	Higher education	All Mobilised in Higher Education (*SupSolidaire*) platform	Collaboration, Leadership	Content focus, Active learning and collaboration, School embedded
Ireland	Schools	Induction programme, release days for school leaders and extra teaching staff	Well-being	Content focus, School embedded
Ireland	Higher education	Reflecting and learning through stakeholder consultations	Leadership	Active learning and collaboration
Korea	Schools	National community of teachers and the Knowledge Spring	Collaboration, Leadership	Content focus, Active learning and collaboration, Sustained duration
Turkey	Higher education	Distance Education Centres in public higher education institutions	Leadership	Active learning and collaboration, Sustained duration, School embedded

Note: Recognising the wide and varied implications that policies have on education policy eco-systems, the selected policies for this table have been coded according to the key policy levers of responsiveness and resilience, and key policy components of which they make direct use.
Source: For descriptions of these initiatives and sources by country, see Annex 7.

As in the pre-crisis period, the majority of the policies selected here are content-focused, generally supporting educators in shifting to online education, or developing capacity so they can perform news sets of tasks. In this way, they help respond to an urgent need for specific skills. In **Chile**, the Online Learning for Teachers portal supports educators in delivering the new Prioritised School Curriculum, which was developed by the ministry after the suspension of in-person classes. In other cases, the programmes focus on building capacity to implement regulatory and practical changes to the way courses and institutions are run. All school teachers in **Ireland** will undertake COVID-19 Induction Training before the start of the new school year to ensure that staff have full knowledge of the latest public health advice and guidance and an outline of the COVID-19 response plan.

Others are able to combine a content focus with opportunity for reflection, which, as explained in the previous section, may encourage deeper engagement. For example, **Colombia** has adapted the Let's all Learn programme, redirecting tutors to accompany teachers of mathematics, language and early years education to adapt their practice for distance education. In **Australia**, as well as publishing guidance online, the Australian Skills Quality Authority (ASQA) offers targeted advice to individual providers moving to online delivery, and plans to conduct a strategic review of online learning in the VET sector by engaging key stakeholders.

Some measures are school-based. Unlike similar initiatives in other countries, where a standardised programme of professional development for school reopening is delivered through national webinars, **Ireland**'s COVID-19 Induction Training is delivered at school level. This aims to help to contextualise national regulations and guidance against the school's specific needs and recovery plans. Another school-embedded approach is **Turkey**'s expansion and strengthening of the Distance Education Centres, which sees additional staff and research assistants placed within higher education institutions to support staff in capitalising on new regulations promoting the digitalisation of higher education. In **France**, an online platform centralises and disseminates initiatives put in place by higher education establishments during the pandemic. Representatives from the institutions submit practices that can then be accessed, adapted and implemented by peers in other institutions.

Several of the selected policies promote collaborative approaches. For some, this is sought through comprehensive stakeholder engagement to inform content. Some examples are the guidance for moving towards distance learning in higher education published by **Ireland**'s National Forum for the Enhancement of Teaching and Learning in Higher Education, and, **Australia**'s new Regulatory Strategy for VET 2020-22. In **Korea**, a national online teacher community of 10 000 teachers, one from every school in the country, aims to promote the sharing of best practice in online education and provides a real-time, interactive communications channel among government and school-based staff. As revealed in the analysis of pre-crisis policies, initiatives that promote collaboration by building strong relationships between different actors within the system can have a positive impact on professional learning while relationship building of this nature can also support policy implementation.

Policies that promote active learning are less common, however. **Chile**'s distance mentoring for management teams is the only example identified here. This initiative includes three video sessions: first, a needs diagnosis; then introduction of targeted support; and finally, an opportunity for reflection.

In terms of building educator resilience, several of the selected policies aim to balance professional learning with well-being measures. For example, **Ireland**'s COVID-19 Induction Training and **Colombia**'s Let's all Learn programme specifically support staff in implementing new policy measures in an effort to relieve some of the implementation burden placed on those on the front line. Furthermore, **Ireland** is also providing funding to allow school leaders to have one release day from teaching per week during the next academic year in recognition of the increased workload derived from adapting to new measures implemented as a result of the pandemic.

Other policies have the potential to foster resilience through promoting the leadership of learning. While **Chile**'s mentoring for school management teams aims to directly strengthen school leadership, other initiatives promote all educators to becoming leaders by positioning them as the drivers of their own learning. This is the case in **France**'s All Mobilised in Higher Education platform and **Korea**'s online community of teachers and the Knowledge Spring, where educators determine the content of their professional learning and design learning opportunities for their colleagues. In this way, these policies also encourage collaboration between professionals across the system. The guidance for moving towards distance learning in higher education published by **Ireland**'s National Forum for the Enhancement of Teaching and Learning in Higher Education directly gives voice to the educators delivering online learning.

This is also an effective way of valuing institutional actors and their professional knowledge, which, as seen in the pre-crisis policies selected for this paper, can help professional learning initiatives succeed by further motivating and engaging educators in their professional practice.

Online delivery may be helping to scale up initiatives. Several policy evaluations from the pre-crisis period highlight the challenge of scaling up policies to have a wider reach. The specific context of the crisis, which has driven a greater use of online delivery, may have helped to overcome this. For example, the online guidance and training programmes delivered through **Colombia**'s Let's all Learn programme will reach 4 500 institutions across the country, **Korea**'s teacher community involves almost every school in the country, and **France**'s online platform already collates over 700 initiatives. At the same time, however, lessons from the pre-crisis period also indicate a need to design policies that address needs at a local level and that are responsive to demand. In this way, **Chile**'s video mentoring programme strikes a good balance: the learning opportunity is tailored to the needs of each participating team, but by being delivered remotely, it can reach a much greater number of participants than in-person visits would allow. In addition, as well as scaling up provision, efforts to ensure accessibility will be key and require careful monitoring of participation and experiences.

Some reflections on common challenges ahead

Generally, across the policies selected here, very few will have a sustained duration beyond the crisis recovery period, with several being one-off training opportunities. As previously discussed, this is not always the most effective approach to professional learning and is less likely to shift practice in the long term. Nevertheless, there are some examples of how policy makers can build more longevity into professional learning initiatives. By establishing new formal institutional structures, **Turkey** hopes to ensure that any positive impact or new learning derived from the experience of emergency distance education is incorporated into future institutional development for the longer term. Based on successful outcomes of **Korea**'s online teacher community, the Ministry of Education will continue the support for a cohort of educational innovators, who will become the driving force behind artificial intelligence and future-driven education post-crisis. Finally, **Australia**'s two-year regulatory strategy provides a focus and a vision for the support offered to providers of VET over the coming years, helping to establish some continuity in support for the transition to increased online learning.

Delegates at the *Education Policy Reform Dialogues 2020* noted that there exists alongside sustaining the duration of professional learning opportunities the ongoing challenge posed by the need for teachers to keep up with rapidly evolving skills demands, as well as an ever-expanding multitude of available learning resources and tools. Possible solutions included putting central guidance in place to help teachers navigate resources and building professional communities of practice to foster horizontal collaboration that can be a constant source of support, adapting to the needs of the changing context.

Policy pointers

This section has explored the ways in which policy efforts in the second half of 2020 may best support educators to develop the new skills and methods required to strengthen educator resilience for the longer term. Taking into account the specific needs of the current context, as well as the lessons learned from pre-crisis policy efforts and recently implemented initiatives for professional learning, three policy pointers for action emerge:

1. Position educators to become the drivers of their own learning

International evidence and policy analysis indicate that professional learning that is clearly aligned with the everyday professional practice of educators can be particularly effective. Creating opportunities for educators to determine or influence the content of their professional learning helps facilitate such alignment while also signalling a higher sense of value for the profession. Furthermore, approaches that position educators as the drivers of their own learning also develop a sense of leadership, which helps strengthen educator resilience. This does not mean leaving educators to their own devices, but rather creating the conditions in which they understand their own development goals, can select from a variety of quality relevant learning opportunities, and have access to the necessary resources and support mechanisms to take full advantage of them. Furthermore, continuously monitoring the effectiveness of professional learning approaches, and listening to educators' needs and experiences will help ensure that opportunities remain relevant even as educators' working contexts change.

2. Provide educators with tools that are responsive to their specific needs and contexts

Teaching is a highly differentiated profession: aspects such as education level, type of delivery, location, and sector play an important role in defining the specific needs of different educators. Considering education level only, international evidence suggests that, compared to school-level educators, professionals working in higher education and vocational settings may have less access to systematic, formal professional learning. Policy analysis further suggests that one-size-fits-all approaches to professional learning are not as effective as more targeted efforts. Therefore, given the specific challenges posed by the COVID-19 crisis to pedagogical staff working in upper secondary and post-secondary general or vocational education, policy makers should consider implementing more tailored approaches, in active collaboration with education institutions. To develop tools that effectively address teachers' diverse professional learning needs and contexts, governments could develop self-assessment instruments (e.g. in digital competence), teacher networks focusing on peer assessment of needs, or more systematised efforts to gain feedback from them on an ongoing basis.

3. Foster collaborative relationships among educators for triple impact

International evidence indicates that professional learning opportunities designed around collaboration with other professionals can be particularly effective at enhancing skills. At the same time, analysis of policy efforts in the pre-crisis period reveals that strong relationships have been key to the effective implementation of successful professional learning policies. Furthermore, collaborative relationships are a powerful driver of educator resilience, promoting creative thinking and experimentation, as well as enhancing working conditions. Therefore, putting relationship building at the centre of policy efforts related to professional learning can simultaneously help to build educators' capacities and strengthen their resilience.

Other relevant OECD work

Insights from this OECD work can also help support policy makers' responses in the current context:

- The OECD Teachers' Professional Learning (TPL) Study combines country-specific diagnoses and international comparative research to identify policies that effectively support the professional growth of teachers. It is designed to provide policy makers with rapid feedback, improve the evidence base and facilitate international peer learning on both initial teacher preparation and continuing professional learning in its various forms. Insights from the TPL study can help countries build professional learning systems that are capable of preparing, supporting and equipping all teachers in the context of rapid change (see **Annex 8**).

References

Arad Research and ICF Consulting (2018), *Formative Evaluation of the Pioneer School Model: Final Report*, Welsh Government, Cardiff, https://gov.wales/statistics-and-research/formative-evaluationpioneer-school-model/?lang=en (accessed on 13 October 2020). [17]

Beltman, S., C. Mansfield and A. Price (2011), "Thriving not just surviving: A review of research on teacher resilience", *Educational Research Review*, Vol. 6/3, Elsevier, Amsterdam, pp. 185-207, http://dx.doi.org/10.1016/j.edurev.2011.09.001. [1]

Boeskens, L., D. Nusche and M. Yurita (2020), "Policies to support teachers' continuing professional learning: A conceptual framework and mapping of OECD data", *OECD Education Working Papers*, No. 235, OECD Publishing, Paris, https://dx.doi.org/10.1787/247b7c4d-en. [8]

Darling-Hammond, L., M. Hyler and M. Gardner (2017), *Effective Teacher Professional Development*, Learning Policy Institute, Palo-Alto, https://learningpolicyinstitute.org/sites/default/files/product-files/Effective_Teacher_Professional_Development_REPORT.pdf (accessed on 13 October 2020). [14]

Elsevier (ed.) (2007), "Teachers resilience: A necessary condition for effectiveness", *Teaching and Teacher Education*, Vol. 23/8, pp. 1302-1316, http://dx.doi.org/10.1016/j.tate.2006.06.006. [2]

Kangas-Dick, K. and E. O'Shaughnessy (2020), "Interventions that promote resilience among teachers: A systematic review of the literature", *International Journal of School & Educational Psychology*, Vol. 8/2, Taylor and Francis Ltd., Abingdon-on-Thames, pp. 131-146, http://dx.doi.org/10.1080/21683603.2020.1734125. [3]

Ministry of Education, Ontario (2019), *New Teacher Induction Program: Induction Elements Manual 2019*, Publications of the Government of Ontario, Toronto, http://www.edu.gov.on.ca/eng/teacher/pdfs/NTIPInductionElements2019.pdf (accessed on 13 October 2020). [16]

OECD (2020), "Coronavirus special edition: Back to school", *Trends Shaping Education Spotlights*, No. 21, OECD Publishing, Paris, https://dx.doi.org/10.1787/339780fd-en. [5]

OECD (2020), "Education Policy Outlook: Czech Republic", *Education Policy Outlook Country Profiles* OECD Publishing, Paris, http://www.oecd.org/education/policy-outlook/country-profile-Czech-Republic-2020.pdf (accessed on 13 October 2020). [18]

OECD (2020), "Education Policy Outlook: Latvia", *Education Policy Outlook Country Profiles* OECD Publishing, Paris, http://www.oecd.org/education/policy-outlook/country-profile-Latvia-2020.pdf (accessed on 13 October 2020). [19]

OECD (2020), "Education Policy Outlook: Portugal", *Education Policy Outlook Country Profiles* OECD Publishing, Paris, http://www.oecd.org/education/policy-outlook/country-profile-Portugal-2020.pdf (accessed on 13 October 2020). [20]

OECD (2020), *Resourcing Higher Education: Challenges, Choices and Consequences*, Higher Education, OECD Publishing, Paris, https://dx.doi.org/10.1787/735e1f44-en. [10]

OECD (2020), *TALIS 2018 Results (Volume II): Teachers and School Leaders as Valued Professionals*, TALIS, OECD Publishing, Paris, https://dx.doi.org/10.1787/19cf08df-en. [11]

OECD (2019), *Education Policy Outlook 2019: Working Together to Help Students Achieve their Potential*, OECD Publishing, Paris, https://dx.doi.org/10.1787/2b8ad56e-en. [15]

OECD (2019), "TALIS 2018", *TALIS (database)*, OECD Publishing, Paris, https://www.oecd.org/education/talis/talis-2018-data.htm (accessed on 13 October 2020). [12]

OECD (2019), *TALIS 2018 Results (Volume I): Teachers and School Leaders as Lifelong Learners*, TALIS, OECD Publishing, Paris, https://dx.doi.org/10.1787/1d0bc92a-en. [13]

OECD (2018), *Education Policy Outlook 2018: Putting Student Learning at the Centre*, OECD Publishing, Paris, https://dx.doi.org/10.1787/9789264301528-en. [9]

Reimers, F. and A. Schleicher (2020), *Schooling Disrupted, Schooling Rethought: How the COVID-19 Pandemic is Changing Education*, OECD Publications, Paris, https://www.educatemagis.org/wp-content/uploads/documents/2020/07/document.pdf (accessed on 13 October 2020). [4]

Révai, N. (2020), "What difference do networks make to teachers' knowledge?: Literature review and case descriptions", *OECD Education Working Papers*, No. 215, OECD Publishing, Paris, https://dx.doi.org/10.1787/75f11091-en. [6]

Viac, C. and P. Fraser (2020), "Teachers' well-being: A framework for data collection and analysis", *OECD Education Working Papers*, No. 213, OECD Publishing, Paris, https://dx.doi.org/10.1787/c36fc9d3-en. [7]

3. Addressing learning gaps now will minimise disruption in students' educational journeys

About this lesson: Disruption to education systems during the COVID-19 pandemic has disproportionately affected the most vulnerable learners, exacerbating pre-existing inequalities with potentially dramatic and long-lasting implications. This requires urgent action to address learning gaps and ensure smooth and continued educational pathways for all learners. Over the longer term, systems will need to strengthen learner resilience, fostering environments in which every individual has the competences required to reach their full potential. To that end, this lesson explores how policy makers can design and implement policy efforts that address these two urgent and important tasks concurrently, effectively implementing remedial measures today while building students' resilience for tomorrow.

In Brief

Resilient education systems have the capacity to respond to the needs of all learners, including the most vulnerable. Such responsiveness may entail timely and effective personalised interventions, additional instruction or resources, or a more targeted allocation of resources. Alongside this, key policy levers to strengthen learner resilience – student well-being, home-school links, capacity building, and evaluation and assessment components – will help all today's learners navigate the even more volatile path they face today. Successful policy experiences from the pre-crisis period show that interventions can benefit from the synergies between these policy components for responsiveness and levers for resilience, especially when initiatives focus on adaptation to the local context and meaningful relationship building. More recent related policy efforts introduced in response to the COVID-19 pandemic show a willingness among policy makers to dedicate additional resources to students in greater need of support, and to build capacity among educators to provide this support. However, the need to capitalise on parental support and ensure a longer-term commitment to intervention programmes also emerges. These findings inform three policy priorities for action that aim to guide policy makers in addressing learning gaps effectively while also strengthening learner resilience.

Infographic 3.1. Lesson 3 and policy pointers for action

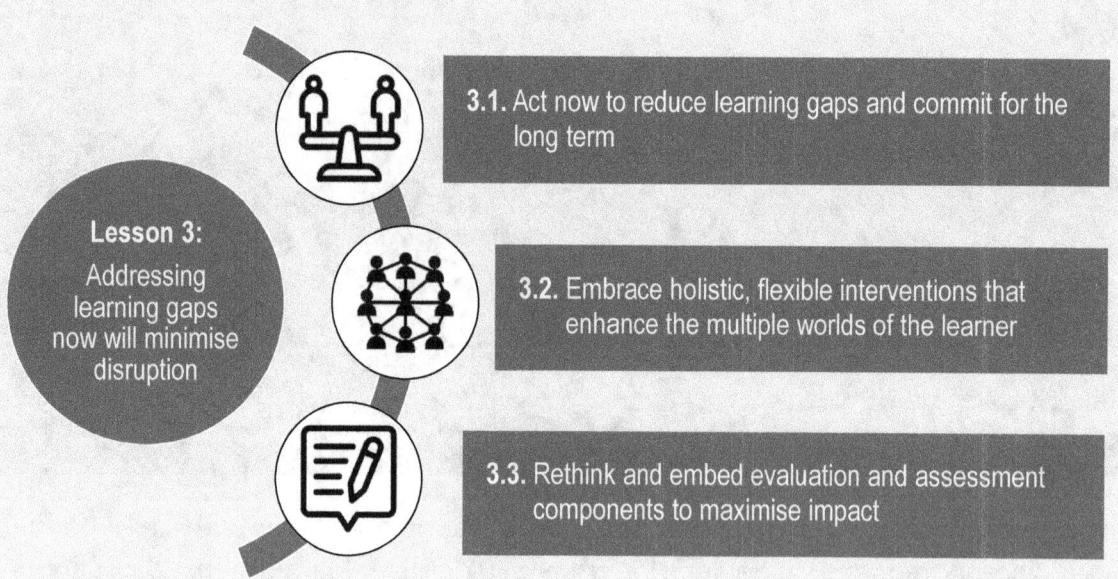

Associated resources (See Annexes)

- Annex 9. Policies addressing learning gaps from the pre-crisis period with evidence of positive impact;
- Annex 10. Selected current policy efforts to address learning gaps;
- Annex 11. Recent work from the OECD's Strength through Diversity project in the context of the COVID-19 pandemic.

Background: Why now?

The crisis brings new urgency to the challenges of equity and learner resilience

A community's resilience lies in its capacity to care for its most vulnerable members, effectively allocating resources to where they are most needed (Ungar, 2011[1]). The COVID-19 crisis has revealed that, when education systems are not resilient in this way, disruptions disproportionately affect the most vulnerable learners with potentially dramatic and long-lasting implications for individuals and societies. To mitigate such damage, education systems must simultaneously address learning gaps and strengthen learner resilience.

By the end of June 2020, more than half of OECD countries had closed schools for at least three months as part of efforts to contain the pandemic (Schleicher, 2020[2]). Despite the range and scope of emergency education measures, national and international estimates point to widening gaps in learning among students (Maldonado and De Witte, 2020[3]; Dorn et al., 2020[4]; World Bank Group, 2020[5]). This corresponds with previous research indicating that students' skills, knowledge and engagement are likely to deteriorate during extended absence from education or forced disruption (e.g. due to the summer break, prolonged teacher strike action or natural disasters) (Gibbs et al., 2019[6]; Jaume and Willén, 2019[7]; Kuhfeld and Tarasawa, 2020[8]).

Indeed, the effects of such closures are not felt equally among students. During periods of home-based education, students' individual needs, their parents' skills and the household resources available to them have a considerable impact on learning. For example, in the COVID-19 crisis, students with an immigrant background whose parents may lack proficiency in the language of instruction, and those with educational needs or disabilities that require specialist support, face extra challenges due to remote learning. Likewise, reliance on digital education can hinder students in rural or remote locations with less reliable digital infrastructure, and those in vocational programmes unable to develop practical skills remotely – an issue exacerbated by a decline in work-based learning opportunities (World Bank Group, 2020[5]; OECD, 2020[9]). Students from low socio-economic backgrounds may also be at a triple disadvantage, with a home environment less conducive to learning, lower access to digital tools, and greater vulnerability to the health and financial impacts of the pandemic. The intersectionality of these vulnerabilities further exacerbates learning gaps for certain students. These gaps need to be addressed immediately, but education systems will also need to consider how to support learners who have home and community environments that are less conducive to learning to benefit from more flexible approaches to the delivery of learning in the longer term.

Even as educational institutions reopen, equity challenges persist. The economic and health impacts of the pandemic will likely create newly vulnerable children. Moreover, as institutions open and close according to viral trajectory, the habit of attending class may be broken and some students could disengage from their learning and their peers. This could increase rates of school dropout and early school leaving, particularly among disadvantaged students (OECD, 2020[10]; Di Pietro et al., 2020[11]). The risk may be even higher at tertiary level, as increased financial and situational constraints deter students from returning to campus or discourage new enrolments among low-income groups (World Bank, 2020[12]).

In many ways, such challenges are not new; individual circumstances over which students have no control (e.g. place of birth, home language or parents' occupations) have long been strong predictors of educational achievement in many OECD countries (OECD, 2019[13]). However, these latest disruptions put today's young people on an unusually volatile path, potentially resulting in lower career earnings across their lifetimes (OECD, 2020[14]; Hanushek and Woessmann, 2020[15]). This means that returning to the status quo is not an option: education systems have the dual task of recovering learning losses and inequalities exacerbated by the emergency response to the COVID-19 crisis while driving education into a better normal where all students are able to thrive, irrespective of their circumstances.

Lesson one of this handbook explored the need for policy makers to enhance resilience in education generally, and to ensure smooth educational pathways that allow each student to reach their own individual potential. In the short term, this requires addressing gaps exacerbated by the pandemic as a matter of urgency; in the longer term, systems need to strengthen learner resilience. Lesson three explores how policy makers can design and implement policy efforts that address these two challenges simultaneously, effectively implementing remedial measures while also building students' resilience. What do we already know about minimising learning gaps and enhancing learner resilience? What related policy efforts are education systems implementing in the second half of 2020 and how can they be strengthened?

Evidence

To support education systems in addressing learning gaps and minimising disruption to students' educational journeys, this section offers highlights of relevant international evidence about learner resilience and bridging learning gaps. Based on evidence of evaluations from selected policies already in place before the pandemic, it also offers insights for policy makers into policy levers and approaches that can promote resilience in students, as well as some ongoing challenges. The section also looks into a selection of relevant policies implemented in the context of the COVID-19 pandemic.

What does international evidence say about learner resilience and remediating gaps?

Resilient learners have a strong capacity to adapt to and overcome the challenges they face (OECD, 2019[13]). Over recent decades, the question of learners' academic resilience (defined by PISA as the share of the most disadvantaged students who are also high-performing) and wider socio-emotional resilience, has attracted a lot of policy attention and research interest. This provides a strong knowledge base for action and, although progress in reducing learning inequalities has been mixed for OECD countries, there is some good news for policy makers.

Firstly, we know that improving equity does not necessarily require high educational spending. Rather, the key lies in allocating resources in a targeted manner (Schleicher, 2019[16]). Secondly, we know that governments do not have to sacrifice excellence in the name of equity; rather, resilience reflects both quality and equity, which some education systems have successfully enhanced simultaneously. Between 2009 and 2018, Ireland and Slovenia reduced the share of low performers and increased the share of high performers in reading while also ensuring that performance increased most substantially among the most disadvantaged students (OECD, 2019[17]; OECD, 2019[13]). Both countries are also relatively low spenders on education: in 2017, Ireland and Slovenia dedicated a lower share of national wealth to educational institutions (primary to tertiary) than on average across the OECD (OECD, 2020[9]).

With the right support, then, student resilience can be strengthened over time. Building on previous OECD and other international research, the Education Policy Outlook's Framework of Responsiveness and Resilience identifies key policy levers that help establish the conditions under which individuals facing adversity may reach a higher level of well-being and academic achievement. These elements are particularly relevant for the shorter term, as countries work to adapt the current academic year to emerging needs. Firstly, understanding and enhancing the various worlds of the student is crucial. This includes **strengthening student well-being**, through either improving students' non-cognitive skills or mind-set, or ensuring a positive learning climate (Agasisti et al., 2018[18]; OECD, 2018[19]). Secondly, **adapting evaluation and assessment components** for greater real-time clarity emerges as relevant good practice, including realistic but ambitious goal setting at system, school or student level; identifying target students and diagnosing learning needs; and monitoring student progress to ensure interventions remain pertinent and sufficient over time. Moreover, **capacity building** among educators enables teachers and other staff who directly administer support to identify and address learning difficulties more effectively. It can also help educators foster positive attitudes among disadvantaged students (OECD, 2018[19]). Finally, enhancing

home-school links is crucial as resilient students tend to benefit from greater parental involvement in their learning (OECD, 2011[20]).

OECD data offers some insight into aspects of student resilience in the pre-crisis period. For example, while aspects related to student well-being generally garner quite positive responses across the OECD, there appears to be room to improve the way in which students are empowered to use evaluation and assessment to become the drivers of their own learning, as well as on capacity building efforts to help strengthen student resilience. Given the current need for focused efforts to address learning gaps and recover losses, combining our knowledge about building student resilience with what we know about effective remediation could help policy makers achieve some quick wins in this area (See Figure 3.1).

Figure 3.1. Several policy levers for student resilience require strengthening across the OECD

Selected indicators of student resilience in the pre-crisis period (2018)

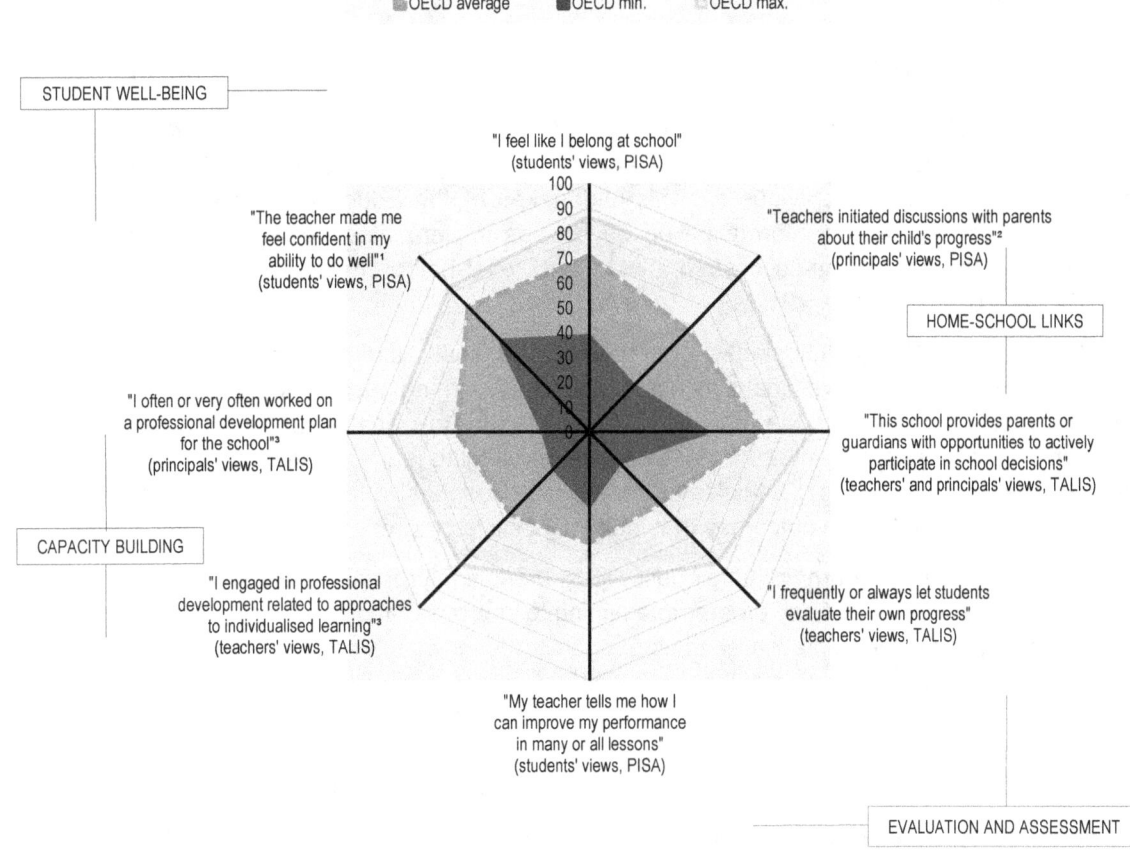

Notes: Indicators related to teachers refer to the responses of lower-secondary teachers; indicators related to students or principals refer to the responses of 15-year-olds, or their school principals. (1) During the previous two language-of-instruction lessons; (2) During the previous academic year; (3). During the 12 months prior to the survey.
Sources: (OECD, 2019[21]), *PISA 2018 Database*, Table III.B1.9.1, Table III.B1.6.2, Table III.B1.10.1, Table V.B1.8.2, Table III.B1.6.3, https://www.oecd.org/pisa/data/2018database/; (OECD, 2019[22]), *OECD TALIS 2018 Database*, Table I.2.6, Table I.5.18, Table II.5.12, https://www.oecd.org/education/talis/talis-2018-data.htm (accessed 19 November 2020).

How do education systems effectively address learning gaps? Across previous OECD work on equity in education, three key policy components of initiatives to address learning gaps emerge:

- **Personalised learning interventions:** A personalised approach to learning is highly sensitive to individual needs and highly adapted to differences between learners (Istance and Dumont, 2010[23]). This does not mean that learning becomes a solitary endeavour based on individual preferences. It means that both collaborative and autonomous learning opportunities respond to the needs of each learner, under the guidance of learning goals defined by education systems. Intervention approaches of this nature include developing individualised development and learning plans, providing one-on-one or very small group coaching or tuition, and, for older students, providing flexible learning options, pathways and transitions for older students.
- **Additional or specialised instruction for certain students:** In order to address a particular need at the individual or small group level, education systems may increase instructional time or employ specially trained professionals (OECD, 2016[24]).
- **Additional resources based on student needs:** To address inequalities in a way that is more cost-efficient or in the context of resource constraints, education systems can direct additional financial or human resources where demand is highest, equalising opportunities for learning and achievement (OECD, 2018[19]).

What can we learn from successful policies to address learning gaps already in place?

Building on the insights of effective practices for strengthening learner resilience and addressing learning gaps offered by international evidence, policy analysis can help illustrate how such initiatives can be planned and implemented. In previous analysis undertaken by the Education Policy Outlook across 43 education systems, it collected information on 59 policies implemented between 2008 and 2019 that focused on supporting education success for all students; over half of these targeted specific population groups (OECD, 2018[25]; OECD, 2019[26]).

In 2020, the Education Policy Outlook has undertaken further analysis of these policies in order to identify examples of policies and initiatives that successfully address learning gaps while potentially strengthening learner resilience. Table 3.1 lists the main policies selected for this analysis. These all benefit from key policy components aligned with international evidence on bridging learning gaps, as well as policy levers identified by the Education Policy Outlook's Framework for Responsiveness and Resilience in education. There are also policy evaluation outcomes that indicate positive progress towards policy objectives.

What common traits can we learn from their policy implementation processes? Firstly, flexibility stands out as an important characteristic of any programme aiming to improve outcomes for a specific student group. Flexibility in design or implementation enables support to better match need. For example, school-level actors surveyed about the implementation of **Chile**'s Preferential School Subsidy appreciated the introduction of more room to modify or adjust school improvement plans throughout the school year (Irarrazaval et al., 2012[27]). In **Estonia**, staff in the Pathfinder Centres are able to adopt a needs-based approach thanks to flexibility in the various intervention mechanisms on offer (CIVITTA, 2017[28]).

This flexibility is also achieved through another commonly cited strength of these policies: the local or even personal nature of interventions. For example, bringing the focus of control to the school or local level, in policies such as those implemented in **Germany** and **Portugal**, appears to have enabled actors who have a connection to the social space of the target group to design bottom-up solutions based on local diagnosis (Verdasca, n.d.[29]; Prognos, 2016[30]). This can also be achieved on a more personalised basis. In **Norway**, the Certificate of Practice Scheme was found to be most successful where thorough assessment of individual cases preceded admission to the scheme; based on the assessments, suitable alternatives are suggested for students for whom the programme is not deemed suitable (CEDEFOP, n.d.[31]). The evaluations of several policies also emphasise the importance of involving the target group in the programme design or implementation. In **Australia** and **Germany**, for instance, this appears to have helped build more genuine, collaborative and sustainable partnerships as well as a stronger understanding of needs and contexts (Department of the Prime Minister and Cabinet, Australia, 2019[32]; Prognos, 2016[30]).

Table 3.1. Pre-crisis policy examples to address learning gaps with evidence of positive impact

Education system	Education level	Policy and year	Policy levers for responsiveness and resilience	Key policy components
Australia	Schools	National Indigenous Reform Agreement (2007)	Student well-being, Evaluation/assessment mechanisms, Capacity building	Additional resources, Specialised/additional support
Australia	Higher education	Higher Education Participation and Partnerships Programme (2010)	Student well-being, Evaluation/assessment mechanisms, Capacity building	Additional resources
Nova Scotia (Canada)	Schools	Schools Plus programme (2008)	Student well-being, Home-school links	Specialised/additional support, Personalised interventions
Chile	Schools	Preferential School Subsidy (2008)	Student well-being, Evaluation/assessment mechanisms, Capacity building	Additional resources
Estonia	Schools	Pathfinder Centres (2015)	Student well-being, Evaluation/assessment mechanisms, Capacity building, Home-school links	Specialised/additional support, Personalised interventions
Finland	Schools / VET	National Core Curricula for Preparatory Instruction (2015)	Student well-being, Capacity building, Home-school links	Specialised/additional support, Personalised interventions
Finland	Schools	Student Welfare Act (2013)	Student well-being, Home-school links	Specialised/additional support, Personalised interventions
Germany	Schools	Education Alliances (2013)	Student well-being	Additional resources
Ireland	Schools	Delivering Equality of Opportunity in Schools Plan (2005, updated 2017)	Student well-being, Evaluation/assessment mechanisms, Capacity building	Additional resources
Norway	VET	Certificate of Practice scheme (2016)	Evaluation/assessment mechanisms, Home-school links	Additional resources, Specialised/additional support, Personalised interventions
Portugal	Schools	National Programme to Promote Educational Success (2016)	Student well-being, Evaluation/assessment mechanisms, Capacity building	Additional resources, Specialised/additional support
Slovenia	Schools	Policies to support the integration of Roma students in schools (2008, 2011, 2016)	Student well-being, home-school links	Specialised/additional support, Personalised interventions

Note: Recognising the wide and varied implications that policies have on education policy eco-systems, the selected policies for this table have been coded according to the key policy levers of responsiveness and resilience, and key policy components of which they make direct use.
Source: For descriptions of these policies, sources and further references by country, see Annex 9.

Indeed, establishing meaningful relationships between service providers and targeted students and their families is seen to be critical. Several evaluations, including those for policies implemented in **Germany**, **Nova Scotia** (Canada) and **Portugal**, note that it is through these relationships that new dynamics and innovations develop and that efficiencies can be made (Verdasca, n.d.[29]; Crinean, Donnelly and LeBlanc, 2012[33]; Prognos, 2016[30]). In **Norway**, the school's active role in the programme was a key feature of success identified in evaluations as it allowed a close relationship both between schools, staff and students, and between schools, staff and the enterprises (CEDEFOP, n.d.[31]). In both **Finland** and **Slovenia**, disseminating information to marginalised learners and their families succeeds best, where delivery is ensured personally by a designated case worker so that stronger relationships can develop (Ministry of Education and Culture, Finland, 2016[34]; Council of Europe, 2017[35]).

Some reflections on common challenges ahead

Common challenges also come into focus. There is a need for coherent, complementary actions, as well as sustained efforts over a longer period. The challenges facing target groups tend to be multi-dimensional and extremely complex, and cannot be overcome through one initiative. In several cases, these policies have been running for more than ten years and have undergone several iterations, with goals, inputs and outputs adapting over time. These modifications are informed by evidence and feedback gathered through ongoing monitoring and evaluation efforts, as in the cases of those policies implemented in **Australia** and **Ireland** (Department of the Prime Minister and Cabinet, Australia, 2019[32]; Weir and Kavanagh, 2019[36]). Indeed, in **Australia**'s Higher Education Participation and Partnerships Programme, the main recommendation of policy evaluation was to develop a stronger evaluation framework through which data could inform future improvements (ACIL Allen Consulting, 2017[37]).

A related challenge found in several of these policies is the need to estimate more carefully the need or demand for additional support, and consequently the necessary resources, especially in terms of time. This is more evident in institution-based interventions such as **Chile**'s Preferential School Subsidy, where the implementation burden lies predominantly with pedagogical staff (Irarrazaval et al., 2012[27]). The challenge for policy makers lies in finding the appropriate balance between establishing a level of local autonomy that enables responsiveness and ensuring adequate capacity and fair workloads among implementation actors.

Finally, a challenge identified in several of the evaluations, including those for the selected policies implemented in **Finland**, **Ireland** and **Nova Scotia** (Canada), relates to ensuring consistency in quality across institutions, municipalities and regions (Crinean, Donnelly and LeBlanc, 2012[33]; Suvi Skantz (14 March 2018), 2018[38]; Weir and Kavanagh, 2019[36]). To some extent, quality differences are inevitable given the local or personal nature of many of these interventions and their ultimate aim to facilitate social change processes, which are inherently non-linear. However, some evaluations suggest that stronger oversight and directing capacity building where it is most needed could help limit such variations.

In related discussions at the *Education Policy Reform Dialogues 2020*, delegates noted that to support more consistency, building engagement and buy-in among implementation actors is important. Delegates noted that this requires ensuring that the initiative offers a clear practical value for those actors themselves and that this value is communicated effectively. It also requires understanding and adapting to the pre-existing assessment culture and keeping in mind that assessment approaches may need to differ for different groups of students. With learner well-being in mind, education systems may need to re-calibrate assessment cultures- particularly high-stakes assessment- although maintaining assessment is necessary to truly understand the impact of crisis and subsequent remediation efforts.

What can we learn from efforts to address learning gaps during the crisis?

> ▶ See Annex 10. Selected current policy efforts to address learning gaps

During the COVID-19 crisis, in both the initial phase of disruption and the current phase of recovery, overcoming learning gaps has played a prominent role in the response of education systems. In the first instance, ensuring all learners had access to new forms of educational delivery was the focus.

With most countries mobilising digital resources to provide distance education, several systems introduced initiatives to provide digital devices to disadvantaged students. For example, as schools closed, **Latvia** conducted a rapid survey to establish the number of children without access to a device or the internet. In partnership with two private companies, the Ministry of Education and Science then donated over 5 000 smart devices in the first week of closures (OECD, 2020[39]).

As the period of closure became more prolonged, specific supports were introduced for certain groups of children. In **Norway**, based on evidence that immigrant communities were particularly vulnerable during the pandemic, students with an immigrant background were prioritised for school-based learning, alongside children of key workers (OECD, 2020[40]). In **Turkey**, the Ministry of National Education developed a mobile application providing content targeted towards students with special educational needs and their parents and teachers. Provincial call centres were established to enable teachers to support and communicate with children with special educational needs and their families (OECD, 2020[41]). As education systems move into the recovery phase, addressing learning gaps remains a key feature of plans for reopening educational institutions. In a recent OECD-Harvard survey, 89% of senior government officials and education administrators responded that plans for school reopening definitely include arrangements to assess and remediate learning gaps for students in general. Among teachers and school administrators, the share was slightly lower, at 66%. The key student groups targeted for remedial measures included those transitioning from one education phase to another, those unable to access online learning and disadvantaged students (Reimers and Schleicher, 2020[42]).

The Education Policy Outlook also conducted desk-based research to identify promising initiatives implemented to address learning gaps planned for implementation in the second half of 2020. The selected policies focus on supporting students to catch up on lost learning as they return to in-person teaching, or to overcome learning gaps, either through the provision of additional resources, specialised or additional support, and/or personalised approaches to learning.

They also incorporate at least one of the identified policy levers from the Framework for Responsiveness and Resilience (student well-being, home-school links, evaluation and assessment components, and capacity building). In total, nine policies were selected, all of which focused on schools, with four including provisions for vocational students at upper secondary or post-secondary level, and none focused on higher education (see Table 3.2 and Annex 10).

Table 3.2. Promising policy initiatives to address learning gaps implemented in 2020

Education system	Education level	Policy	Policy levers for responsiveness and resilience	Key policy components
Chile	Schools	Tutors for Chile	Capacity building	Specialised/additional support, Personalised interventions
Chile	Schools & VET	Comprehensive Assessment of Learning and curricular prioritisation	Student well-being, Evaluation/assessment mechanisms, Capacity building	Additional resources
France	Schools & VET	National benchmarking assessments and additional resources	Student well-being	Additional resources, Specialised/additional support, Personalised interventions
Japan	Schools	Reinforcing human resources in schools	Student well-being, Home-school links	Additional resources, Specialised/additional support
Netherlands	Schools & VET	Catch-up programmes for the academic year 2020/21	Student well-being, Capacity building, Home-school links	Additional resources
Portugal	Schools	School Action Plans for the Recovery and Consolidation of Learning	Student well-being, Evaluation/assessment mechanisms, Capacity building	Additional resources, Specialised/additional support, Personalised interventions
England (United Kingdom)	Schools	Catch-up Premium	Student well-being, Capacity building	Additional resources, Personalised interventions
England (United Kingdom)	Schools & VET	National Tutoring Programme	Student well-being, Capacity building	Specialised/additional support, Personalised interventions
Wales (United Kingdom)	Schools	Recruitment of extra teachers and teaching assistants	Evaluation/assessment mechanisms, Capacity building	Additional resources, Specialised/additional support, Personalised interventions

Note: Recognising the wide and varied implications that policies have on education policy eco-systems, the selected policies for this table have been coded according to the key policy levers of responsiveness and resilience, and key policy components of which they make direct use.
Source: For descriptions of these initiatives and sources by country, see Annex 10.

The majority of policies analysed for this document aim to address learning gaps by mobilising additional funds, to be used by education institutions with some degree of autonomy. In other countries, educational institutions will receive additional financial resources to dedicate to providing extra support to certain students. **England**'s (United Kingdom) Catch-up Premium, a one-off, universal payment of GBP 80 per student in mainstream schools and GBP 240 for those in special education settings or alternative provision for 2020/21 aims to ensure that schools have sufficient resources to help all students make up for lost teaching time. Schools will receive additional funds in three instalments across the academic year and are encouraged to pool resources to prioritise support according to student need. Schools and secondary VET institutions in the **Netherlands** can apply for government subsidies to run voluntary interventions between 2020 and 2021. These may take the form of after-school programmes, catch-up programmes during school holidays or extra support during the school day.

However, while additional resources can be helpful for education institutions, other types of support can also help to make a difference. A majority of selected initiatives also include efforts to build capacity among educators; this is particularly positive given the unprecedented nature of institutional closures and their unpredictable impact on students' learning. Some of these are formal approaches to professional development: in **Chile**, professional mentors observe trainee teachers during tutoring sessions with students and provide feedback on their professional practice. In another Chilean initiative, school management teams can access video mentoring sessions to support the implementation of diagnostic assessments. Other policies include more informal approaches to capacity building through disseminating international evidence and best practice: the Education Endowment Foundation, **England**'s (United Kingdom) What Works Centre for education has conducted rapid evidence reviews and produced accessible guides to support schools in making evidence-based spending decisions for the Catch-up Premium. Similarly, in the **Netherlands**, the Ministry provides schools with research summaries to support catch-up programme design.

Others aim to increase access to specialised or additional support in order to help certain students recover lost learning. This can also help educational staff already in place to focus on a more rounded strategy for student success. For example, **Wales** (United Kingdom) will recruit additional teachers and teaching assistants throughout 2020/21 to support students in the final years of secondary education, as well as disadvantaged and vulnerable learners of all ages. **France** is increasing the hours of support available in the first months of the school year through educational assistants and individual support with homework, and the government has doubled a previous commitment by creating 8 000 new support posts for students with disabilities. In **Japan**, extra school counsellors and social workers have been assigned on a school-by-school basis, according to need.

Indeed, a large number of selected policies encourage educators to implement personalised interventions to address students' learning needs. This may take the form of small group or one-on-one tuition as in the **England**'s (United Kingdom) National Tutoring Programme (to be launched in November 2020) or coaching and mentoring as in **Wales**' (United Kingdom) deployment of extra staff for students at the end of upper secondary education and **Portugal**'s promotion of peer mentoring within schools.

Pairing personalised approaches with evaluation and assessment efforts to meet students' needs appears a particularly promising approach. **Chile**, **France** and **Portugal** have all implemented comprehensive initiatives to ensure that schools diagnose students' learning needs on the return to in-person teaching. In **Chile**, this involves specifically designed assessments that cover both cognitive and non-cognitive skills, while **France** has adapted pre-existing testing arrangements as well as introducing new assessments for the beginning of the academic year. **Portugal** encourages all schools to identify students' needs, beginning with an assessment of students' digital skills and the digital resources available to them, then using curricular documents and essential learning objectives to map where the gaps in learning are. Finally, some countries are providing additional pedagogical tools to support educators in bridging learning gaps. New student assessment tools in **Chile** and curriculum planning tools in **Portugal** aim to support schools to prioritise learning tasks in the first weeks of in-person teaching.

A smaller number of selected policies also support students' well-being or foster a positive learning environment. **Japan** and **Portugal** have both increased the availability of school-based support professionals, such as school counsellors and social workers, while **Chile**'s diagnostic assessments include an assessment of students' socio-emotional skills. However, given the considerable and ongoing threats posed by the COVID-19 pandemic to students' physical and mental health, and to their engagement in education and attendance at school, it is likely that efforts to improve students' well-being will be increasingly relevant. Establishing an environment – both internal and external – that is conducive to learning is critical to the success of any educational intervention programme.

Some reflections on common challenges ahead

Among the selected policies, intentions to engage parents in initiatives to address learning gaps were less clearly set out, however. This causes concern for three reasons. Firstly, as seen in the pre-crisis policy experiences, key characteristics of success in policies that address learning gaps include strong relationships between the different actors involved and a strong connection to the social space of the target student; parents are essential to this. Secondly, it is important to capitalise on the elevated role of parents in their children's education during institutional closures; often acting as *de facto* instructors during that period, parents may be able to offer valuable insights into students' needs. Finally, given the unpredictability of the virus' trajectory, further institutional closures may yet occur, in which case, the parents' role will once again be central to children's learning.

All such efforts must be sustainable over the longer term. One reason is that the very real possibility of future institutional closures means that interventions implemented as schools reopen must be flexible enough to endure future emergency scenarios by remaining deliverable through remote means. This will help ensure that learning gaps are not further exacerbated in the short term. Another reason is that, as seen in the pre-crisis period, efforts to redress learning inequalities benefit from being implemented over a sustained period, both to allow them time to overcome the adjustments of initial implementation processes, and to hone and strengthen approaches in response to monitoring data. This will also help to avoid underestimating the scale of demand and the resources required, which was a common pitfall in policies addressing learning inequalities during the pre-crisis period.

Further related challenges were raised in discussions at the *Education Policy Reform Dialogues 2020*. Delegates highlighted that confronting deepening educational inequalities requires embracing the contributions of all stakeholders, including parents, but also staff, students and actors within the wider education community. In particular, delegates discussed the need to avoid treating these as disparate stakeholder groups, recognising them as part of an educational community and taking advantage of the synergies between them. Delegates also emphasised the importance of policy evaluation and monitoring mechanisms as a means of improving the impact of interventions, noting that assessment cancellations in response to the virus should be avoided in order to enable systems to continue to generate valuable data. Nonetheless, keeping student well-being in mind, such efforts should remain low-stakes for students themselves.

Policy pointers

Lesson three has explored the ways in which policy efforts in the second half of 2020 may best address learning gaps to minimise short and long-term disruption to children's education. Taking into account the specific needs of the current context, as well as the lessons learned from pre-crisis policy efforts and recently implemented initiatives to address learning gaps, three policy pointers emerge:

1. Act now to reduce learning gaps and commit for the long term

The closure of educational institutions will have been challenging for the vast majority of students, and particularly so for those from vulnerable population sub-groups, exacerbating learning gaps that already existed. If not addressed now, these inequalities may increase as the crisis period continues, and will have significant social and financial implications for individuals and societies in both the short and long term.

At the same time, previous experience indicates that learning inequalities are too complex to be remedied quickly. Several of the most effective pre-crisis policies considered for this analysis had been in place for more than a decade. Furthermore, the effects of the COVID-19 crisis are likely to be felt well beyond the reopening of education institutions. Therefore, students need urgent support to bridge learning gaps, but governments must also aim for long-term commitment.

2. Embrace holistic, flexible interventions that enhance the multiple worlds of the learner

Incorporating flexibility into policy design enables implementation actors to better tailor intervention and remediation efforts to the needs of the target audience and to changing contextual demands. Mechanisms of flexibility may include shifting the focus of control to the institution or local level, bringing together professionals with different specialisms to tailor interventions, or providing the tools and resources to enable the use of a variety of delivery methods.

Similarly, education systems need to adopt approaches that take into account the ways in which the different worlds of a student intersect in order to shape his or her learning experience. Approaches include strengthening student well-being, developing a more positive learning climate within education institutions, and enhancing home-school links to establish an educational student-centric eco-system that is conducive to learning and receptive to extra support. Involving students and parents in the design and delivery of learning interventions is a particularly useful way of achieving this.

3. Rethink and embed evaluation and assessment components to maximise impact

In contexts of disruption, it is critical to ensure that learners, the broader education community and the system can monitor learning progress in a timely manner and adapt pedagogical processes accordingly. Prior to introducing remedial measures, diagnostic assessments are essential in ensuring that students' needs are fully met. As the student receives support, ongoing formative assessment provides opportunities for powerful feedback loops to both student and educator. Finally, ongoing monitoring and evaluation efforts of the policy itself at institutional and system level will help hone the approach to optimise impact.

Other relevant OECD work

Insights from this OECD work can also help support policy makers' responses in the current context:

- The *Strength through Diversity project* is conducting further analysis to support policy makers to develop equitable and inclusive education systems (see **Annex 11**). Insights from this work can also help support policy makers shape responses in the context of the COVID-19 pandemic.

References

ACIL Allen Consulting (2017), *Evaluation of the Higher Education Participation and Partnerships Programme*, ACIL Allen Consulting, Melbourne, https://docs.education.gov.au/system/files/doc/other/final_heppp_evaluation_report_2017.03.16_0.pdf (accessed on 13 October 2020). [37]

Agasisti, T. et al. (2018), "Academic resilience: What schools and countries do to help disadvantaged students succeed in PISA", *OECD Education Working Papers*, No. 167, OECD Publishing, Paris, https://dx.doi.org/10.1787/e22490ac-en. [18]

CEDEFOP (n.d.), *Certificate of Practice (Praksisbrev)*, European Center for the Development of Vocational Training, Brussels, http://www.cedefop.europa.eu/en/printpdf/toolkits/vet-toolkit-tackling-early-leaving/resources/certificate-practice-praksisbrev (accessed on 13 October 2020). [31]

CIVITTA (2017), *Mid-term Evaluation of the Study and Career Guidance Programme: Final Report*, CIVITTA – The Challenge Advisory, Tartu, http://dx.doi.org/www.hm.ee/sites/default/files/aruanne_1.pdf (accessed on 13 October 2020). [28]

Council of Europe (2017), *Fourth Report Submitted by Slovenia Pursuant to Article 25, Paragraph 2 of the Framework Convention for the Protection of National Minorities*, Council of Europe, Strasbourg, https://rm.coe.int/CoERMPublicCommonSearchServices/DisplayDCTMContent?documentId=09000_016806d3fbc (accessed on 13 October 2020). [35]

Crinean, K., G. Donnelly and S. LeBlanc (2012), *Evaluation of Schools Plus – Year Three Final Report*, Collective Wisdom Solutions, Halifax, https://www.ednet.ns.ca/schoolsplus/en/files-schoolsplus/sp_evaluation-year3-final-september24.pdf (accessed on 13 October 2020). [33]

Department of the Prime Minister and Cabinet, Australia (2019), *Closing the Gap Report 2019*, Australian Government, Canberra, https://antar.org.au/sites/default/files/2019_ctg_report.pdf (accessed on 13 October 2020). [32]

Di Pietro, G. et al. (2020), *The likely impact of COVID-19 on education: Reflections based on the existing literature and recent international datasets*, Publications Office of the European Commission, Luxembourg, https://publications.jrc.ec.europa.eu/repository/bitstream/JRC121071/jrc121071.pdf (accessed on 13 October 2020). [11]

Dorn, E. et al. (2020), *COVID-19 and student learning in the United States: The hurt could last a lifetime*, McKinsey & Company, New York, https://www.mckinsey.com/~/media/McKinsey/Industries/Public%20Sector/Our%20Insights/COVID-19%20and%20student%20learning%20in%20the%20United%20States%20The%20hurt%20could%20last%20a%20lifetime/COVID-19-and-student-learning-in-the-United-States-FINAL.pdf (accessed on 13 October 2020). [4]

Gibbs, L. et al. (2019), "Delayed Disaster Impacts on Academic Performance of Primary School Children", *Child Development*, Vol. 90/4, pp. 1402-1412, http://dx.doi.org/10.1111/cdev.13200. [6]

Hanushek, E. and L. Woessmann (2020), "The economic impacts of learning losses", *OECD Education Working Papers*, No. 225, OECD Publishing, Paris, https://dx.doi.org/10.1787/21908d74-en. [15]

Irarrazaval, I. et al. (2012), *Evaluation of the first years of Implementation of the Preferential School Subsidy*, Centre for Public Policy, Pontifical Catholic University of Chile, Santiago,, http://www.researchgate.net/publication/320735176_Evaluacion_de_los_primeros_anos_de_Implementacion_del_Programa_de_Subvencion_Escolar_Preferencial_de_la_Subsecretaria_de_Educacion?enrichId=rgreq-7866d6507a522842331bcfed8e20ebf8-XXX&enrichSource=Y292ZXJQYWdlOzMyMDczNTE3NjtBUzo1NTU4OTM2NDExODMyMzJAMTUwOTU0Njc4MDEwOA%3D%3D&el=1_x_2&_esc=publicationCoverPdf (accessed on 13 October 2020). [27]

Istance, D. and H. Dumont (2010), "Future directions for learning environments in the 21st century", in *The Nature of Learning: Using Research to Inspire Practice*, OECD Publishing, Paris, https://dx.doi.org/10.1787/9789264086487-15-en. [23]

Jaume, D. and A. Willén (2019), "The Long-Run Effects of Teacher Strikes: Evidence from Argentina", *Journal of Labor Economics*, Vol. 37/4, University of Chicago Press, Chicago, pp. 1097-1139, http://dx.doi.org/10.1086/703134. [7]

Kuhfeld, D. and D. Tarasawa (2020), "The COVID-19 slide: What summer learning loss can tell us about the potential impact of school closures on student academic achievement", *Collaborative for Student Growth*, Northwest Evaluation Association, Portland, https://www.nwea.org/content/uploads/2020/05/Collaborative-Brief_Covid19-Slide-APR20.pdf (accessed on 13 October 2020). [8]

Maldonado, J. and K. De Witte (2020), "The effect of school closures on standardised student test outcomes", *Discussion Paper Series*, No. DPS20.17, KU Leuven Department of Economics, Leuven, https://feb.kuleuven.be/research/economics/ces/documents/DPS/2020/dps2017.pdf (accessed on 13 October 2020). [3]

Ministry of Education and Culture, Finland (2016), *The Educational Tracks and Integration of Immigrants – Problematic Areas and Proposals for Actions*, Publications of the OKM, Helsinki, http://julkaisut.valtioneuvosto.fi/bitstream/handle/10024/64986/okm6.pdf (accessed on 13 October 2020). [34]

OECD (2020), "Combatting COVID-19's effect on children", *OECD Policy Responses to Coronavirus (COVID-19)*, http://www.oecd.org/coronavirus/policy-responses/combatting-covid-19-s-effect-on-children-2e1f3b2f/ (accessed on 13 October 2020). [10]

OECD (2020), *Education at a Glance 2020: OECD Indicators*, OECD Publishing, Paris, https://dx.doi.org/10.1787/69096873-en. [9]

OECD (2020), "Education Policy Outlook: Latvia", *Education Policy Outlook Country Profiles* OECD Publishing, Paris, http://www.oecd.org/education/policy-outlook/country-profile-Latvia-2020.pdf (accessed on 13 October 2020). [39]

OECD (2020), "Education Policy Outlook: Norway", *Education Policy Outlook Country Profiles* OECD Publishing, Paris, http://www.oecd.org/education/policy-outlook/country-profile-Norway-2020.pdf (accessed on 13 October 2020). [40]

OECD (2020), "Education Policy Outlook: Turkey", *Education Policy Outlook Country Profiles* OECD Publishing, Paris, http://www.oecd.org/education/policy-outlook/country-profile-Turkey-2020.pdf (accessed on 13 October 2020). [41]

OECD (2020), "Youth and COVID-19: Response, recovery and resilience", *OECD Policy Responses to Coronavirus (COVID-19)*, http://www.oecd.org/coronavirus/policy-responses/youth-and-covid-19-response-recovery-and-resilience-c40e61c6/ (accessed on 13 October 2020). [14]

OECD (2019), *Education Policy Outlook 2019: Working Together to Help Students Achieve their Potential*, OECD Publishing, Paris, https://dx.doi.org/10.1787/2b8ad56e-en. [26]

OECD (2019), "PISA 2018", *PISA* (database), OECD Publishing, Paris, https://www.oecd.org/pisa/data/2018database/ (accessed on 13 October 2020). [21]

OECD (2019), *PISA 2018 Results (Volume I): What Students Know and Can Do*, PISA, OECD Publishing, Paris, https://dx.doi.org/10.1787/5f07c754-en. [17]

OECD (2019), *PISA 2018 Results (Volume II): Where All Students Can Succeed*, PISA, OECD Publishing, Paris, https://dx.doi.org/10.1787/b5fd1b8f-en. [13]

OECD (2019), "TALIS 2018", *TALIS (database)*, OECD Publishing, Paris, https://www.oecd.org/education/talis/talis-2018-data.htm (accessed on 13 October 2020). [22]

OECD (2018), *Education Policy Outlook 2018: Putting Student Learning at the Centre*, OECD Publishing, Paris, https://dx.doi.org/10.1787/9789264301528-en. [25]

OECD (2018), *Equity in Education: Breaking Down Barriers to Social Mobility*, PISA, OECD Publishing, Paris, https://dx.doi.org/10.1787/9789264073234-en. [19]

OECD (2016), *Low-Performing Students: Why They Fall Behind and How To Help Them Succeed*, PISA, OECD Publishing, Paris, https://dx.doi.org/10.1787/9789264250246-en. [24]

OECD (2011), *Against the Odds: Disadvantaged Students Who Succeed in School*, PISA, OECD Publishing, Paris, https://dx.doi.org/10.1787/9789264090873-en. [20]

Prognos (2016), *Culture Makes you Strong: Education Alliances Report on the Evaluation Period 2014-2015*, Federal Ministry of Education and Research, Germany, http://www.bmbf.de/files/Bericht%20Evaluation%202014-2015%20final.pdf (accessed on 13 October 2020). [30]

Reimers, F. and A. Schleicher (2020), *Schooling Disrupted, Schooling Rethought: How the COVID-19 Pandemic is Changing Education*, OECD Publications, Paris, https://www.educatemagis.org/wp-content/uploads/documents/2020/07/document.pdf (accessed on 13 October 2020). [42]

Schleicher, A. (2020), "The Impact of COVID-19 on Education: Insights from Education at a Glance 2020", https://www.oecd.org/education/the-impact-of-covid-19-on-education-insights-education-at-a-glance-2020.pdf (accessed on 13 October 2020). [2]

Schleicher, A. (2019), *PISA 2018: Insights and Interpretations*, OECD Publications, Paris, https://www.oecd.org/pisa/PISA%202018%20Insights%20and%20Interpretations%20FINAL%20PDF.pdf (accessed on 13 October 2020). [16]

Suvi Skantz (14 March 2018) (2018), "Extensive evaluation: pupil and student welfare has been enhanced after the enforcement of the Pupil and Student Welfare Act, but the development work is far from over", *Finnish Education Evaluation Center*, https://karvi.fi/en/2018/03/14/extensive-evaluation-pupil-student-welfare-enhanced-enforcement-pupil-student-welfare-act-development-work-far/ (accessed on 13 October 2020). [38]

Ungar, M. (2011), *Community resilience for youth and families: Facilitative physical and social capital in contexts of adversity*, Elsevier, Amsterdam, http://dx.doi.org/10.1016/j.childyouth.2011.04.027. [1]

Verdasca, J. (n.d.), *National Programme for the Promotion of School Success: Presentation Note*, https://pnpse.min-educ.pt/programa (accessed on 13 October 2020). [29]

Weir, S. and L. Kavanagh (2019), *The Evaluation of DEIS at Post-Primary Level: Closing the Achievement and Attainment Gaps*, Educational Research Centre, Dublin, http://www.erc.ie/wp-content/uploads/2019/01/Weir-Kavanagh-2018-DEIS-post-primary.pdf (accessed on 13 October 2020). [36]

World Bank (2020), *The COVID-19 Crisis Response: Supporting tertiary education for continuity, adaptation, and innovation*, World Bank Group, Washington D.C., http://pubdocs.worldbank.org/en/808621586532673333/WB-Tertiary-Ed-and-Covid-19-Crisis-for-public-use-April-9-FINAL.pdf (accessed on 13 October 2020). [12]

World Bank Group (2020), "TVET Systems' response to COVID-19: Challenges and Opportunities", http://documents1.worldbank.org/curated/en/930861589486276271/pdf/TVET-Systems-response-to-COVID-19-Challenges-and-Opportunities.pdf (accessed on 13 October 2020). [5]

4. Annexes: Associated resources for policy makers

About this section: This section groups selected resources for policy makers in the form of 11 annexes. These annexes also support the analysis undertaken in this handbook for **Lesson 1 (Annexes 1-5)**, **Lesson 2 (Annexes 6-8)** and **Lesson 3 (Annexes 9-11)**.

Annex 1. Links to government sources on delivery methods in the second half of 2020

This table collates the sources consulted for the information presented in Figure 1.2 (*Delivery methods for the second half of 2020 (primary and secondary education)*) and Figure 1.3 (*Delivery methods for the second half of 2020 (post-secondary education)*) of Lesson 1. The sources pertaining to post-secondary education generally refer to higher education, however, some relate to post-secondary, non-tertiary institutions. The date refers to the date of publication or, where this is not available, the date the information was accessed.

Due to the rapidly changing nature of the current situation, some of the information in this table may be subject to more recent updates. Figure 1.2 and Figure 1.3 are therefore best interpreted as representing the intended or preferred mode of delivery from September 2020.

Table 4.1. Sources consulted for information about delivery methods in the second half of 2020

Country	Education Level	Source	Date
Australia	Schools	Australian Health Protection Principal Committee (AHPPC) advice on reducing the potential risk of COVID-19 transmission in schools	26 April 2020
	Post-secondary	Coronavirus (COVID-19) – latest regulatory advice	10 September 2020
Austria	Schools	Corona traffic lights in schools and elementary educational institutions	17 August 2020
	Post-secondary	Coronavirus (COVID-19)	15 September 2020
Belgium	Schools	Flemish Community: Scenario 2020-2021: regular and special primary education Scenario 2020-2021: regular secondary education, buso OV3 - OV4 and HBO5 French Community: Organisation of Courses and / or Regulatory Information German-speaking Community: Ministerial Circular Education And Child Care, What Measures Apply to Primary and Secondary Schools?	08 July 2020 September 2020 24 July 2020 28 September 2020 05 November 2020
	Post-secondary	Flemish Community: Roadmap 2020-2021: universities French Community: Organisation of Courses German-speaking Community: www.ostbelgienbildung.be/coronavirus	11 September 2020 24 August 2020 16 October 2020
Brazil	Schools	School closures and reopenings by country	20 September 2020
	Post-secondary	More than half of the Federal Education Network has remote activities	19 August 2020
Canada	Schools	Alberta: https://open.alberta.ca/publications/2020-21-school-re-entry-plan British Columbia: https://www2.gov.bc.ca/gov/content/education-training/k-12/covid-19-return-to-school#our-plan Manitoba: https://www.manitoba.ca/asset_library/en/covid/k12-guidelines-oct20.pdf Newfoundland and Labrador: https://www.gov.nl.ca/eecd/files/education-re-entry-document.pdf Nunavut: https://gov.nu.ca/education/information/2020-21-opening-plan-nunavut-schools New Brunswick: https://www2.gnb.ca/content/dam/gnb/Departments/ed/pdf/return-to-school-guide.pdf Northwest Territories: https://www.gov.nt.ca/covid-19/sites/covid/files/resources/reopening_nwt_schools_safely_plan_for_2020-21_eng.pdf Nova Scotia: https://novascotia.ca/coronavirus/docs/back-to-school-plan.pdf Ontario: https://www.ontario.ca/page/guide-reopening-ontarios-schools Prince Edward Island: https://www.princeedwardisland.ca/sites/default/files/publications/psb_september_2020_guidelines_10.pdf Québec: https://www.quebec.ca/en/education/back-to-school-plan-fall-covid-19/	September/October 2020

		Saskatchewan: https://www.saskatchewan.ca/government/health-care-administration-and-provider-resources/treatment-procedures-and-guidelines/emerging-public-health-issues/2019-novel-coronavirus/safe-schools-plan Yukon: https://yukon.ca/en/health-and-wellness/covid-19-information/education-and-school-supports-covid-19/planning-2020-21#school-operations-in-the-2020%E2%80%9221-school-yearhttps://peopleforeducation.ca/our-work/tracking-canadas-education-systems-response-to-covid-19/?fbclid=IwAR1V1szLKDG-mdUh0yctv4IOofLB9skiYusISjUI1Uw28gu3YSG_XDv-tuI	
	Post-secondary		
Chile	Schools	Mineduc presents news in the implementation of the School Admission System in the context of COVID-19	28 August 2020
	Post-secondary	MINEDUC Action Plan for Higher Education Institutions	18 March 2020
Colombia	Schools	We are taking steps so that, gradually, classes in schools are resumed with an alternation model, President Duque told the boy Jacobo Faciolince	19 August 2020
	Post-secondary	Ministry of Education issues directive 13 with recommendations for the development of academic activities in practical and research laboratories in Institutions of Higher Education and for Work and Human Development	04 June 2020
Costa Rica	Schools	MEP announces no return to face-to-face classes during 2020	27 August 2020
	Post-secondary		
Czech Republic	Schools	Frequently asked questions about education and coronavirus	01 September 2020
	Post-secondary		
Denmark	Schools	Guidelines and legislation	06 July 2020
	Post-secondary	Information about COVID-19 (Corona virus)	01 August 2020
Estonia	Schools	Spread of COVID-19: recommendations for educational institutions, parents, students	19 August 2020
	Post-secondary	Education, culture, sports	01 July 2020
Finland	Schools	New school year began in contact teaching	13 August 2020
	Post-secondary	Updated recommendations for early childhood education and care, schools, educational institutions and higher education institutions to prevent the spread of the coronavirus	04 August 2020
France	Schools	Resume The Path To Success For All, In The Safety Of Students And Staff	01 September 2020
	Post-secondary	Covid-19: French Higher Education Mobilised	06 August 2020
Germany	Schools	Karliczek: Digital education is a "must have"	13 August 2020
	Post-secondary	HRK Senate: Priority for health protection – as much face-to-face teaching as possible	02 July 2020
Greece	Schools	New conditions for modern distance education: For students and teachers who will be absent due to coronavirus as well as for educational structures under suspension	13 September 2020
	Post-secondary	Measures to prevent the spread of coronavirus COVID-19 in Higher Education Institutions (HEIs) during the period of the re-examination period September of the academic year 2019-2020	21 August 2020
Hungary	Schools	It is possible to start education traditionally on September 1st	25 August 2020
	Post-secondary	Sectoral Recommendations for Organizing Higher Education During the State of Health Crisis	28 September 2020
Iceland	Schools	Q&A about school restrictions due to COVID-19 Regulation on the restriction of school work due to epidemics	03 September 2020 03 November 2020
	Post-secondary	Guidelines for on-site university-level education Restrictions applying to schools and universities from Nov. 3rd	19 September 2020 03 November 2020
Ireland	Schools	Roadmap for the full return to school	27 July 2020

	Post-secondary	Guidance for Further and Higher Education for returning to on-site activity in 2020: Roadmap and COVID-19 Adaptation Framework	29 August 2020
Israel	Schools	Preparations for the opening of the year - August 2020	
	Post-secondary		
Italy	Schools	Adoption of the Document for the planning of school activities, in all institutions of the national education system for the 2020/2021 school year	26 June 2020
	Post-secondary		
Japan	Schools	COVID-19 cases at elementary and junior and senior high schools and the countermeasures based on this data	06 August 2020
	Post-secondary	Survey on the implementation policy of classes in the second semester, etc. at universities, etc.	15 September 2020
Kazakhstan	Schools	On making changes in the order of the Minister of Education and Science of the Republic of Kazakhstan from August 13, 2020 ? 345	13 August 2020
	Post-secondary	On making changes in the order of the Minister of Education and Science of the Republic of Kazakhstan from August 13, 2020	13 August 2020
Korea	Schools	Plans for 2nd Semester Announced (2020-07-31)	31 July 2020
	Post-secondary	National information provided to the Education Policy Outlook in ongoing work with the Ministry of Education.	October 2020
Latvia	Schools	For 2020/2021. school year	15 September 2020
	Post-secondary	Recommendations for universities and colleges for implementing precautions to limit the spread of the Covid19 infection	01 August 2020
Lithuania	Schools	Minister of Education A. Monkevicius: lessons in schools will be held in accordance with safety requirements Another Eight Municipalities Put Under Quarantine	25 August 2020 28 October 2020
	Post-secondary	National Reforms in Higher Education	14 September 2020
Luxembourg	Schools	Schools, foyers scolaires and crèches	25 May 2020
	Post-secondary		
Mexico	Schools	School closures and reopenings by country	20 September 2020
	Post-secondary	Bulletin No. 208 SEP Announces Dates of Admission Process and Beginning of Higher Education Courses	16 August 2020
Netherlands	Schools	COVID-19 and the education sector	15 June 2020
	Post-secondary	Frequently Asked Questions about COVID-19 and higher education	01 September 2020
New Zealand	Schools	Advice for schools/kura	14 September 2020
	Post-secondary	Guidelines for Tertiary Education Organisations on how to operate under different Alert Levels	01 September 2020
Norway	Schools	Information about the coronavirus outbreak and kindergartens, schools and higher education	09 September 2020
	Post-secondary	Information about the coronavirus outbreak and kindergartens, schools and higher education	09 September 2020
Poland	Schools	Coronavirus information and recommendations: information for students	31 August 2020
	Post-secondary	New Academic Year at Polish Universities with Safety Measures	19 October 2020
Portugal	Schools	National Reforms in School Education	08 September 2020
	Post-secondary	Covid-19	Warnings	04 August 2020
Slovak Republic	Schools	B. Gröhling: The school year should start on 2 September at each school	21 August 2020
	Post-secondary		
Slovenia	Schools	September 1, all pupils and students of the school are ready for the beginning of the school	27 August 2020

		year	
	Post-secondary	Kindergartens and schools open their doors on Monday	15 May 2020
Spain	Schools	The Ministries of Health and Education and FP finalize the guide of recommendations for the academic year 2020-21, after the contributions of the Autonomous Communities	27 August 2020
	Post-secondary	Recommendations Of The Ministry Of Universities To The University Community To Adapt The Course University 2020-2021 To An Adapted Presentiality And Action Measures Of The Universities In A Case Suspect Or One Positive Of Covid-19	31 August 2020
Sweden	Schools	For educational actors, teachers and students due to covid-19	15 September 2020
	Post-secondary	For educational actors, teachers and students due to covid-19	15 September 2020
Turkey	Schools	Minister Selçuk Explains Face To Face Education Which Is Set To Begin On September 21 During A Live Tv Program	11 September 2020
	Post-secondary	New normalization process in global epidemic	30 July 2020
England (United Kingdom)	Schools	Guidance for full opening: schools	17 September 2020
	Post-secondary	Higher education: reopening buildings and campuses	15 September 2020
Northern Ireland (United Kingdom)	Schools	Weir updates guidance on use of face coverings in schools	25 August 2020
	Post-secondary	Coronavirus (COVID-19): advice on schools, colleges and universities	28 August 2020
Scotland (United Kingdom)	Schools	Coronavirus (COVID-19): guidance on re-opening school age childcare services	21 August 2020
	Post-secondary	Coronavirus (COVID-19): universities, colleges and student accommodation providers	11 September 2020
Wales (United Kingdom)	Schools	Back to school plans from September: coronavirus Coronavirus Firebreak Guidance	01 September 2020 19 October 2020
	Post-secondary	Higher education and student support: coronavirus	15 September 2020

Annex 2. Links to governments' main system-level guidelines for the second half of 2020

This table collates the sources consulted for the information presented in Figure 1.4 (*Education systems' efforts to adapt pedagogical practices in the current academic year: Mapping according to the main guidelines produced by ministries for education delivery*). The sources selected for analysis are system-level guidelines, in place at either primary, secondary or post-secondary level, which have a pedagogical focus. Due to the rapidly changing nature of the current situation, some of the information in the guidelines may be subject to more recent updates.

Table 4.2. System-level guidelines consulted for information about shifting pedagogical practices in the second half of 2020

Country	System-level guideline consulted	Date of publication
Australia	3 Step Framework for a Covid Safe Australia	n.d.
	Resumption planning: continuing delivery in a changed world	n.d.
Austria	Digitisation in schools: 8-point plan for digital education	19 June 2020
	COVID-19 Guidelines for Secure University Operations	August 2020
Belgium	Flemish Community: Corona Measures: Frequently Asked Questions - Schools	31 August 2020
	French Community: Back to School Strategy September 2020/21 in the Context of COVID-19 – Basic Education and Back to School Strategy September 2020/2021 in the Context of COVID-19 - Secondary	19 August 2020
		18 August 2020
	German-speaking Community: Ministerial Circular Education And Child Care: COVID-19	17 July 2020
Brazil	Reorganisation of the School Calendar due to COVID-19 Pandemic	28 April 2020
Canada	Alberta: 2020/21 School Re-entry Plan	27 August 2020
	Manitoba: Welcoming our Students Back: K-12 Guidelines for September 2020	30 July 2020
	Nova Scotia: Nova Scotia's Back to School Plan	22 July 2020
	Ontario: Guide to re-opening Ontario's Schools	30 July 2020
	Prince Edward Island: Welcome Back to School Plan	30 June 2020
Chile	Guidance for Implementation of the Curricular Prioritization in Remote Form and Face-to-face	July 2020
Colombia	Guidelines for the Provision of the Service of Education at Home and Onsite Learning	June 2020
Costa Rica	Guidelines for educational intervention in educational centers against COVID - 19	March 2020
Czech Republic	School operation manual: reopening	27 August 2020
Denmark	Guidelines for primary and lower secondary schools as well as youth and adult education in the area of the Ministry of Children and Education	19 June 2020
	Guidelines for continuing education, independent vocational schools and boarding schools at independent and private schools at the Ministry of Children and Education area in connection with prevention of the spread of COVID-19	19 June 2020
Estonia	Key activities for the academic year 2020/21	n.d.
Finland	Organising basic education from 1.8.2020	01 August 2020
	Provision of vocational training from 1.7.2020	01 July 2020
France	Back to School 2020: Practical information	August 2020
	Back to School 2020: Pedagogical Priorities and Positioning Tools for September and October	August 2020
	Guidelines for MESRI Operators Regarding the Start of the University Year 2020	06 August 2020
Germany	Coronavirus pandemic: For a crisis-resistant education system	5 August 2020
Hungary	Recommendation on possible methods and tools of education without face-to-face meetings	25 August 2020
	Action Plan A 2020/2021: The Academic Year In Public Institutions - Preparedness Procedures (V3)	01 October 2020
	Good practices for Higher Education Institutions in relation to distance education	01 September 2020
Ireland	COVID-19 Response Plan for the safe and sustainable reopening of Primary and Special Schools	27 July 2020
		27 July 2020
	COVID-19 Response Plan for the safe and sustainable reopening of Post Primary Schools-	29 August 2020

Country	Document	Date
	Guidance for Further and Higher Education for Returning to Onsite Activity in 2020: Roadmap and Covid Adaptation Framework	
Israel	Developing resilience in school teams	n.d.
Italy	Guidelines for Hybrid Education	n.d
	Document for the planning of school, educational and training activities in all institutions of the national education system for the 2020/2021 school year.	26 June 2020.
Japan	Education in Japan beyond the crisis of COVID-19 – Leave no one behind	September 2020
	Comprehensive Package for Ensuring Children's Learning in the COVID-19 crisis	05 June 2020
Kazakhstan	About the modification of the order of the Minister of Education and Science of the Republic of Kazakhstan from March 20, 2015 of No. 137 "About the approval of Rules of the organization of educational process on distance learning technologies"	28 August 2020
Korea	Reopening Schools in Korea Amid the Covid-19 Pandemic	09 June 2020
	Q&A on the new online school year	n.d.
Latvia	Recommendations for the organization of the study process in general and vocational education institutions, taking into account the epidemiological situation during Covid-19	01 August 2020
Lithuania	Description of criteria for teaching by distance learning process organization	02 July 2020
	Description of the forms of study according to formal education programs (except for higher education study programs) and the procedure of organizing teaching	03 August 2020
	Description of the procedure for providing social pedagogical assistance to a child and a student	03 August 2020
Mexico	Pedagogical guidelines for the start and organisation of the academic year 2020/21	12 June 2020
Netherlands	Service document for school boards primary education coronavirus COVID-19	14 July 2020
New Zealand	Guidance for school teachers and leaders	August 2020
Norway	Training at home during corona virus situation	23 April 2020
Poland	Coronavirus: information and recommendations	n.d.
Portugal	Guidelines for Recovery and Consolidation Of Learning Academic Year 2020/21	August 2020
	Guidelines for organising the 2020/2021 school year	n.d.
	Recommendations for higher education institutions for the preparation of the academic year	05 August 2020
Slovak Republic		
Slovenia	Education in the Republic of Slovenia under Covid-19	August 2020
Spain	Order EFP / 561/2020, of June 20, which publishes Agreements of the Education Sector Conference, for the initiation and development of the 2020-2021 academic year	20 June 2020
	Recommendations of the Ministry of Universities to the University Community to Adapt the 2020-2021 University Course to Adapted Presence	31 August 2020
Sweden	Rules for preschools and schools that are open or need to close due to the corona pandemic	August 2020
Turkey	Face-to-Face Education, Kindergarten and Primary School Begins in First Grade	21 September 2020
England (United Kingdom)	Guidance for full opening: schools	15 September 2020
	QAA: Preserving Quality and Standards Through a Time of Rapid Change: UK Higher Education in 2020-21	02 June 2020
Northern Ireland (United Kingdom)	Curriculum Planning 2020/21	23 June 2020
Scotland (United Kingdom)	Coronavirus (COVID-19): guidance on preparing for the start of the new school term in August 2020 - version 2	25 August 2020
	Coronavirus (COVID-19): Curriculum for Excellence in the Recovery Phase	05 May 2020
Wales (United Kingdom)	Guidance on Learning in Schools and Settings-Autumn Term: Covid-19	13 June 2020
	COVID-19 Resilience Plan: Strategic Framework for Learning Delivery from September 2020	August 2020
	Covid-19 Resilience Plan for the post-16 sector	September 2020

Annex 3. Mapping of elements from governments' system-level guidelines according to the EPO's Framework for Responsiveness and Resilience in education (in process)

This table classifies information presented in the main system-level guidelines selected for analysis in Lesson one according to the Education Policy Outlook's Framework of Responsiveness and Resilience in Education.

Documents were identified for 37 countries; a full list of sources consulted is available in Annex 2. An overview of the Education Policy Outlook's Framework of Responsiveness and Resilience in Education is presented in the Introduction to the Handbook.

Table 4.3. Classification of information collected through system-level guidelines

STUDENTS		
Understanding and/or Strengthening the Internal World of the Student		AUT, BEL (De., Fl., Fr.), BRA, CHL, ESP, EST, FRA, GBR (NIRL, SCT, WLS), IRL, ISR, NLD, TUR
	Measures to improve well-being at student level	
		Knowledge and skills for social and emotional well-being
		Student voice
		14 countries
Providing Targeted Support and Interventions		AUS, BEL (Fr.), CAN, CHL, COL, CRI, ESP, FIN, FRA, GBR (ENG., NIRL, SCT, WLS), IRL, ISR, JPN, KOR, MEX, NZL, PRT, SVN, TUR
	Personalised and flexible learning for all learners	
	Personalised learning and support for specific needs	
		Promoting inclusive education
		Providing additional or specialised instruction for students with specific needs
		Allocating additional resources based on student needs
		Early intervention
		22 countries
BROADER LEARNING ENVIRONMENT		
Optimising Wider Engagement and Collaboration Within and Beyond the Education Institution		BEL (Fr.), BRA, COL, CRI, DEU, FRA, GBR (SCT), ITA, JPN, KOR, PRT, SVN
	Extended provision and collaboration between public services	
	Bringing together the different environments in which students live and learn	
		Parental engagement
		Employer engagement
		Community engagement
		12 countries
Strengthening Capacity for Adaptation		AUS, AUT, BEL (De), CAN, CHL, DEU, GBR (ENG, WLS), IRL, JPN
	Adapting policies and practices to local context	
	Strengthening the resilience of teachers and school leaders	
		Developing instructional leadership
		Teacher collaboration
		Teacher well-being
		10 countries

SYSTEM

Collecting, Disseminating and Improving the use of Information about Students		AUS, AUT, BEL (De), CAN, CHL, DEU, GBR (ENG, WLS), HUN, IRL, JPN, NZL
	Broader collection of student information	
		Digitisation of assessment
		Holistic view of student progress
		Diagnostic assessment to inform teaching and provide additional support
		Balancing formative and summative forms of assessment
	Improving the dissemination of data on student progress	
	Improving the use of student data	
		By institutions
		By teachers
		By students	12 countries
Developing Smoother and More Permeable Student Learning Pathways		CAN, GBR (WLS), LVA, NLD, NOR, POL, PRT, SVN, SWE
	Ensuring relevance of the educational offer for the labour market	9 countries
		Transition to the workplace through work-based learning
	Smoothing transitions within and beyond the education system	
		Permeability of tracks
		Reducing grade repetition
		Reducing school failure
		Transition from one phase to another
		Flexible entry and exit points
	Supporting students in developing ambitious and realistic career expectations	
		Targeted financial support for students and their families
		Providing information on career and education pathways
Aspects Related to Digitalisation		AUS, AUT, BEL (De., Fl.), BRA, CAN, CHL, CRI, DEU, ESP, FIN, FRA, GBR (ENG, NIRL, SCT), HUN, ITA, JPN, KAZ, KOR, LVA, NLD, NZL, PRT, SVN
	Building capacity for digital learning	
			24 countries

Note: In total, 37 countries were included for analysis. In Canada, education is the exclusive jurisdiction of the provinces and the territories, amongst which there is variation in approaches. For this analysis, five of the provinces and territories were considered.
Source: See Annex 2 for a full list of sources consulted by country.

Annex 4. Recent work from the OECD's Future of Education and Skills 2030 project in the context of the COVID-19 pandemic

The OECD's **Future of Education and Skills 2030** has supported education systems to work together to co-create a vision of the future of education (OECD Learning Compass 2030) and to specify *what* types of knowledge, skills, attitudes and values students need to thrive in and shape their future. The project currently focuses on *how* education systems can enable schools, teachers, other stakeholders and students themselves to be ready to make this future vision a reality. For this, the project takes an *eco-system approach to curriculum redesign and delivery.*

This box provides insight into a key relevant finding of the project during the COVID-19 crisis.

Box 3. The 2nd Virtual Workshop of the Global Forum on the Future of Education and Skills 2030 (8-9 October 2020)

The Second Workshop focused on **reducing equity gaps**. The E2030 participating countries have concurred that the existing equity gaps not only became visible but were also amplified in the midst of the crisis. The discussions focused on addressing: (a) **shrinking curriculum** (what is not learned during school closure and the associated pressure to catch up), and (b) **assessment** (in particular, high-stakes assessment). These challenges were identified as a key barrier to tackling other issues such as **student well-being**, **motivation, school failure** and **school dropout**.

Participants discussed means to address these challenges through: **adjusting curriculum content** for students facing difficulty without stigmatisation or stratification; **adjusting assessment and evaluation**; and **adjusting the role of teachers and teaching**, especially in the context of hybrid delivery models.

From the equity perspective, stakeholders in the field highlighted and re-iterated the effectiveness of **formative assessment with quality feedback**, **instead of high-stakes assessment**, particularly for students at risk. In light of this, some countries have adjusted high-stakes assessments. For example, in **Estonia**, passing state exams was not a condition for graduating from high school this spring, and taking state exams was voluntary. Upon request, high school students could take the state exit exam in mother tongue, in mathematics and one internationally recognised foreign language exam. At the school level, **Ireland** reported that in the case of localised closures, schools are expected to provide remote experiences and broad guidelines provided by the Department of Education to guide schools as to what measures to put in place. There is initial evidence the schools are encouraging greater use of online platforms for the submission of student/pupil work completed at home.

Looking to the future, students shared the types of feedback they welcome from their teachers to maintain their motivation and well-being, while welcoming timely feedback by machines such as AI-chatbots on types of questions where answers are fixed. For teachers to provide the quality feedback students are expecting, they would need proper time and training, as is suggested by the latest PISA data; the percentage of students in schools whose principals reported that teacher mentoring exists in the school varies considerably across countries. Furthermore, the role of students in these conversations also matters as the feedback sessions should not be one-directional. However, a considerable gap is also observed across different systems as to whether or not schools seek student feedback. The project will continue to explore the types of assessments as well as learning environments that can enable better student learning and well-being as we move towards a 'new normal in education'.

Source: OECD (2020), The Global Forum on the Future of Education and Skills 2030: Second Meeting (Virtual Workshop) 8-9 Oct 2020. For more information about this project, please visit: https://www.oecd.org/education/2030-project/.

Annex 5. Recent work from the OECD's Implementing Education Policies project in the context of the COVID-19 pandemic

The OECD's Implementing Education Policies project aims to help countries and jurisdictions close the gap between educational aspirations and performance by providing strategic advice and support in the design and implementation of specific reforms or policies at school level.

This box provides an insight into a key relevant finding of the project during the COVID-19 crisis. It offers further substantive background to the Education Policy Reform Dialogues 2020 Session 1 – *Schools, higher education and Vocational Education and Training (VET): Making the most of resilient approaches in education for a better new normal.*

Box 4. OECD efforts on education policy implementation in the context of the pandemic

For an education policy to be successful and accomplish change in schools, implementation processes need to be well-designed and supported. In times of emergency, such as the COVID-crisis, the speed in the implementation of responses is key, while there may be limited evidence of what can work, as well as binding constraints on resources and capacity. Having a coherent framework for implementing education responses to COVID-19 can save time and result in better outcomes.

The coherent implementation of an education response to COVID-19 that supports equity, quality and well-being can help build school systems' resilience for potential education emergencies and for the future. The OECD toolkit recommends that policy makers consider shaping an actionable implementation strategy with the following dimensions: the involvement of key stakeholders to develop a policy that weaves hybrid approaches to teaching and learning with a clear vision and objectives, generic health and educational guidelines, and the provision of training and support to those in need to manage inequities. Within these national/regional guidelines, autonomy for schools to shape their own approaches needs to rely on education professionals' capacity and available technological resources. The strategy will need to align student assessments and school and system evaluations to the policy. The implementation strategy can weave these actions together, make them actionable, and communicate them in terms of who does what, when, and how, as well as how progress will be measured.

Experience from the first COVID-19 wave showed that many education systems did not have time to shape and implement coherent strategies for the emergency situation. For example, they had not defined a vision for schools beyond closing them physically, leaving them to define their own approaches for continued student learning. Upon the return to schools in September, in many countries, as shown in Annex tables of this handbook, vision and guidelines have been produced, student assessments have been, or are in the process of being, adapted, and more coherent approaches for COVID-19 education responses are in place. This experience can help education systems design processes that can make them more responsive to change.

Sources: OECD (2020), "Education responses to COVID-19: an implementation strategy toolkit", OECD Education Policy Perspectives, No. 5, OECD Publishing, Paris, https://doi.org/10.1787/81209b82-en.
Gouëdard, P., B. Pont and R. Viennet (2020), "Education responses to COVID-19: Implementing a way forward", *OECD Education Working Papers*, No. 224, OECD Publishing, Paris, https://doi.org/10.1787/8e95f977-en.

For more information about this project, please visit: http://www.oecd.org/education/implementing-policies/.

Annex 6. Professional learning policies from the pre-crisis period with evidence of positive impact

This annex provides descriptions and evaluative findings for the policies from the pre-crisis period that were selected for analysis in lesson two. The information comes from previously published material from the Education Policy Outlook which was drafted in consultation with participating education systems. The policies selected focus on professional learning for educators, show evidence of having made positive progress towards policy objectives and make use of key policy levers for educator resilience and responsiveness.

Ontario (Canada): Expansion of New Teacher Induction Programme (2009)

In the province of Ontario, the New Teacher Induction Program (NTIP) aims to support the growth and professional learning of new teachers. It builds upon the first step of initial teacher education and is the second step of on-the-job learning along a continuum of learning and growth for new teachers. The NTIP consists of the following induction elements: 1) orientation for all new teachers with information about the Ontario curriculum and context, and their specific school; 2) professional development and training in areas such as literacy and numeracy strategies and classroom strategies; and 3) mentoring for new teachers by experienced teachers. In addition to the NTIP induction process, new permanent teachers are evaluated twice within their first 12 months of employment through the Teacher Performance Appraisal process. Upon completion of two satisfactory evaluations, a notation reflecting completion of NTIP is placed on the teacher's certificate of qualification and registration that appears on Ontario College of Teachers' public register (OECD, 2019[1]).

Progress or impact: Since 2009, the New Teacher Induction Program has been providing support for first-year, long-term occasional (LTO) teachers with assignments of 97 days or longer. In 2018, the scope of NTIP was expanded to enable school boards to support any teacher in their first five years of practice. The inclusion of these teachers in any of the NTIP induction elements is designed to provide boards with flexibility to respond to local hiring realities and to potentially support new teachers for a greater length of time. Boards may decide to include an entire category of NTIP eligible teachers or base the support they offer on a case-by-case basis. Overall, each year, approximately 8 000 new hired teachers access NTIP support. Including second-year teachers and mentors, the total number of teachers participating in NTIP exceeds 18 000 annually. The results of longitudinal research from 2012 to 2015 show that new teachers have made meaningful and sustained improvements in all four of the core goal areas of NTIP (confidence, efficacy, instructional practice and commitment to ongoing learning) (OECD, 2019[1]).

For more information on progress or impact:

Christine Frank & Associates (2020), *Beginning Teachers' Learning Journeys Longitudinal Study: Year 4 Report*, Christine Frank & Associates/Cathexis Consulting Inc., Toronto, https://www.teachontario.ca/servlet/JiveServlet/downloadBody/11955-102-1-18891/BTLJ-y4-report-final+Eng.pdf (accessed 19 November 2020).

Ministry of Education, Ontario (2019), *New Teacher Induction Program: Induction Elements Manual 2019,* Publications of the Government of Ontario, Toronto, http://www.edu.gov.on.ca/eng/teacher/pdfs/NTIPInductionElements2019.pdf (accessed 19 November 2020).

Denmark: National Corps of Learning Consultants (2014)

The establishment of a national corps of learning consultants (around 40) to support municipalities and schools in enhancing the quality of instruction, beginning in 2014, has been key in the Danish approach to school improvement. They work with schools and municipalities on a host of themes depending on the school year, through webinars or other events, or through intensive counselling and development targeted at schools' specific circumstances – such as in support of the agreement to "fight parallel communities". Under the 2014 *Folkeskole* reform, Learning Consultants also sought to strengthen learning environments and classroom management, through support for teachers, school leaders and municipalities, also with the assistance of various Ministry-developed materials and other networks. Additionally, in 2016 the MoCE allocated DKK 23 million to employ learning consultants from 2016-2019 to support ECEC facilities with a high share of disadvantaged children (OECD, 2020$_{[2]}$).

For more information on progress or impact:

Bjørnholt, B. et al. (2019), Evaluation of the Ministry of Education's Learning Consultant Programme and Activities: Efforts in Primary and Lower Secondary Education, Vocational Training and Upper Secondary Education, Knowledge for Welfare – The National Research and Analysis Centre for Welfare (VIVE), Copenhagen, https://www.uvm.dk/-/media/filer/uvm/aktuelt/pdf-19/191029-evaluering-af-buvm-laringskonsulentforlob-og-aktiviteter.pdf.

Finland: Network of tutor-teachers for basic education (2016)

OKM committed to developing a network of tutor-teachers for basic education. The role is carried out by a teacher who embraces new pedagogies and promotes the digitalisation of teaching. Actions may include organising training on digital pedagogy, conducting competence surveys, providing technical guidance or networking with peers. The initial plan committed to having 2 500 tutor-teachers in schools, providing EUR 23 million to train and support them between 2016 and 2018. A survey of tutor-teachers (2017) concluded that the project had a highly positive impact. A total of 2 289 tutor-teachers were operating across 90% of municipalities by 2018, over 80% of whom had been trained via the government's discretionary transfers. Ongoing challenges include demand for a more regional focus to the tutor network, guidance from OKM as to the competences tutor-teachers should work on and securing a long-term funding strategy. The model has expanded to upper secondary schools, with a focus on supporting the implementation of reforms, including curricular reform. An EC report (2019) found considerable improvements in teachers' digital competencies but ongoing disparities in the integration of digital tools in the classroom. As Finland moved to online learning during the COVID-19 pandemic, this policy may have proved beneficial in both having raised digital competencies among teachers and providing an established support network within and between schools (OECD, 2020$_{[3]}$).

For more information on progress or impact:

Finnish National Agency for Education (EDUFI) (2018), *Tutor Teacher Activities in Basic Education in Finland*, Facts Express 3C/2018, EDUFI, Helsinki, https://www.oph.fi/sites/default/files/documents/195451_oph_faktaa_express_3c_2018_englanti_sivut.pdf.

France: Network of Digital Education Advisors (2014)

France is divided into 30 education academies (or administrative districts) directed by rectors, who implement the national education policies at the regional level and interact with regional stakeholders that share legal educational responsibilities with the Ministry of Education. The digital education advisers advise the rectors of each academy, liaise with local authorities and companies on digital education matters, and lead actions and networks around the uses of digital tools in education. Beyond advising the rectors, they develop projects, actions and training, as well as sharing and mobilising knowledge for teachers to become more active in the use of digital tools for learning. During the COVID-19 crisis, the network of digital education advisorsadvisers worked to ensure the quick transition from in-person to online distance schooling with no day of interruption by:

- working with local authorities to lend and deliver computers and learning worksheets to all students;

- mobilising existing repositories of curated online resources (notably the Digital Educational Resources Platform [BRNE], Eduthèque and Canotech);
- providing online training to teachers and school principals about the availability and use of digital resources for pedagogical practice;
- sharing and promoting of teaching and learning practices adapted to educational continuity and progressive school reopening;
- working with other public education partners on the deployment of their education continuity initiatives, notably the National Centre for Distance Education (CNED) and public TV and radio channels.

The originality of this initiative lies in the mobilisation of a network of education advisors with a good knowledge of past initiatives and strong relationships with all major stakeholders in the field, enabling quick negotiations with partners, rapid communication, and an understanding of the peculiarities of the various local contexts over the French territory (Vincent-Lancrin, 2020[4]).

Ireland: Centre for School Leadership (2015)

The Centre for School Leadership (CSL), a partnership arrangement of the Department for Education and Skills, the Irish Primary Principals' Network and the National Association of Principals and Deputy Principals, has aimed to develop a coherent continuum of professional development for school leaders, initially focusing on coaching, mentoring and pre-service qualification. A postgraduate diploma in school leadership (2017) had 239 graduates in the first cohort and steadily larger annual intakes subsequently. An evaluation of the CSL (2018) found greater recognition of the profession, its role and importance. Beneficiaries of the services reported enhanced confidence, resilience and reflective thinking. Coaching is available for up to 400 principals and leadership teams a year, and every newly-appointed principal can receive mentoring (OECD, 2020[5]).

For more information on progress or impact:

Fitzpatrick Associates (2018), *School Leadership in Ireland and the Centre for School Leadership: Research and Evaluation – Final Report*, Fitzpatrick Associates, Dublin, https://cslireland.ie/images/downloads/Final_CSL_Research_and_Evaluation_Final_Report_Feb_2018_.pdf.

Ireland: National Professional Development Framework for Higher Education (2016)

The National Professional Development Framework (2016) for all higher education teaching staff aims to encourage engagement in professional development, guide CPD choices and support quality assurance. An evaluation of the pilot (2018) commended the transformative potential of engaging with the framework and emphasised the importance of providing staff with space and time to engage in CPD, as well as strong leadership (OECD, 2020[5]).

For more information on progress or impact:

Donnelly, R. and T. Maguire (2018), *Ireland's National Professional Development Framework: Summary Findings from the Initial Implementation*, National Forum for the Enhancement of Teaching and Learning in Higher Education, Dublin, https://www.teachingandlearning.ie/wp-content/uploads/PD_Framework_2018_AW_Web.pdf.

New Zealand: Communities of Learning | Kāhui Ako (2014)

In 2014, New Zealand introduced Communities of Learning | Kāhui Ako (CoLs) as part of the Investing in Educational Success initiative, which aimed to raise educational achievement by improving the quality of leadership and teaching to spread best practice across the school network. This new structural approach to education in New Zealand adopted a networked approach, bringing schools at different levels of the education system together to establish a clearer learner pathway. This approach has aimed to help to overcome issues of school isolation and a lack of collegial networking, previously identified within the school system. The model also aimed to bring together schools to share challenges and goals and to enhance teaching practice and leadership through opportunities for collaborative enquiry and knowledge sharing. Three new professional roles have been introduced: Community Leader, Across-Community of Learning Teacher, and Within School Teacher. These new roles work across and within the community to support and share effective teaching and leadership practice. Since 2014, the Education Review Office has released a range of resources to support the establishment and progress of CoLs (OECD, 2019[1]).

Progress or impact: As of 2018, New Zealand had implemented 214 Communities of Learning, which catered to 1 761 schools, 495 early learning services and 11 tertiary education providers. This constitutes the majority of New Zealand's schools and more than 610 000 students in total. An initial progress report found growing momentum for the establishment of CoLs and high levels of shared purpose and commitment, as well as recognition for the importance of collaboration among professionals. At the same time, a more recent comprehensive consultation process across the education system also collected feedback on a difficulty for schools to step away from the former model that had them in competition with each other. Often, the success of a CoL is highly dependent on the level of skill and commitment among the leadership. As such, experiences are highly varied (OECD, 2019[1]).

For more information on progress or impact:

Ministry of Education of New Zealand (2016), *Uptake and Early Implementation: Communities of Learning | Kāhui Ako*, Ministry of Education of New Zealand, Wellington, https://www.educationcounts.govt.nz/__data/assets/pdf_file/0003/181551/Uptake-and-earlyimplementation-Communities-of-Learning-Kahui-Ako.pdf.

Norway: Advisory Team Programme (2009) and Follow Up Scheme (2017)

In Norway, the Advisory Team Programme (2009) was incorporated into the Follow Up Scheme in 2017 as part of the new competence development model for schools. The programme provides support to schools and school owners that face special challenges in core areas such as quality, literacy and numeracy, and need guidance for school improvement. The programme recruits experienced school leaders and administrators from local governments to support schools and municipalities. It is led by the Directorate of Education and Training, and national partners include the Norwegian Association of Local and Regional Authorities (KS), county governors (who manage national education offices at the county level), the higher education sector, consulting groups and practitioners. School owners manage school development. Others, including principals and local support groups, may also participate depending on the subject (OECD, 2019[1]).

Progress or impact: After an initial pilot in 2009-10, the first regular portfolio of the Advisory Team started in 2011. By 2014, the programme's activities covered 429 municipalities in 18 counties (the whole country except for Oslo). As of 2013, almost 30 municipalities had 80-100 schools in each portfolio, receiving guidance for 18 months. By the end of 2013, the Advisory Team had offered guidance to all municipalities in the country. Initially, many in the education sector viewed the initiative as controversial and resisted the measure: this included school owners, universities and colleges, and public administration. Prior to the Advisory Team, the Directorate of Education and Training and local authorities reportedly did not rely on national guidance as a tool for local development work. Reducing the risk of resistance subsequently required a constant emphasis on the voluntary nature of the initiative. School owners seeking counselling were reminded that their intentions were courageous and beneficial for local education. From the point of view of public administrators, the Advisory Team represented an unnecessary interference of state authorities at the local level. In the higher education sector, the initiative came across as professional competition. Support grew mainly due to its centralised, tight management and the government's efforts to familiarise all actors and stakeholders with the strategy's different aspects. Only advisors who achieved all competency requirements following an obligatory training programme were engaged for the initiative's consultations. By 2013, resistance had almost disappeared at all levels. Support from public administration and the higher education sector increased, and both sectors integrated the initiative into their professional and organisational activities. School owners having received counselling report satisfaction. Advisors also reported satisfaction in seeing the guided municipalities making progress and earning valuable experience and development competence in their own municipalities and schools. Since the incorporation of the Advisory Team Programme into the Follow Up Scheme, in 2017 and 2018, 66 municipalities were selected based on criteria, including standardised tests in literacy and numeracy, final grades after secondary school and results from the Pupil Survey concerning well-being, bullying and motivation. In response, half of the municipalities decided to receive guidance from the Advisory Team Programme, while the other half chose to receive support from other measures. The next selection of municipalities is planned for 2020 (OECD, 2019[1]).

For more information on progress or impact:

OECD (2019), *Improving School Quality in Norway: The New Competence Development Model*, Implementing Education Policies, OECD Publishing, Paris, https://doi.org/10.1787/179d4ded-en.

Portugal: Strengthening the School Association Professional Development Centres (2014)

Much of the ongoing teacher professional development in Portugal is carried out by the 91 School Association Professional Development Centres (Centros de Formação de Associação de Escolas, CFAE) in place across the country. Decree-Law 22/2014 and Decree-Law 127/2015 were passed to clarify the role of the CFAE as formal institutions in order to support the implementation of the new lifelong training framework. This included giving the CFAE greater autonomy in working with local schools and school clusters to determine training needs. These are then integrated into annual or multiannual training plans for the centres which are accredited by the Scientific-Pedagogical Council of Continuing Professional Development. The CFAE recruit a cohort of volunteer teacher-trainers from local schools and tertiary institutions. The OECD (2018) praised the locally responsive nature of the CFAE but found that impact is restricted as too few teachers take advantage of the training, and the offer needs to be better aligned to the priorities of schools and teachers (OECD, 2020[6]).

For more information on progress or impact:

Liebowitz, D., et al. (2018), *OECD Reviews of School Resources: Portugal 2018*, OECD Reviews of School Resources, OECD Publishing, Paris, https://doi.org/10.1787/9789264308411-en.

Sweden: Collaborative research-based learning projects for teachers (2012)

Sweden has introduced pedagogical training initiatives structured as collaborative research-based learning. These "Boost" programmes, for teachers of mathematics, reading and science were launched with a budget of EUR 28 million. The **Boost for Mathematics** (*Matematiklyftet*) programme (2012), for example, is available to all mathematics teachers, tutors and school principals. Materials are produced in collaboration with over 20 Swedish universities and colleges and published on line. Materials are organised according to year groups and school type, and all follow a four-part structure supporting teachers to: 1) prepare independently, using the materials provided to them; 2) meet colleagues to discuss what they have read and collaboratively plan a lesson; 3) teach the lessons in their own classrooms; and 4) reconvene to evaluate and discuss their experiences. Weekly discussion meetings focus on didactic questions and are moderated by mathematics tutors trained by national authorities. During the programme, teachers exchange learning materials, ideas and experiences and enter into professional dialogue. The programme fosters collaborative teaching and enhances teamwork. School principals are also involved (OECD, 2019[1]).

Progress or impact: A final evaluation report (2016) from the Swedish National Agency for Education found that this collegial training model has had a positive impact. Over 35 000 teachers were found to have participated in the mathematics training, which corresponds to 75% of all mathematics teachers in compulsory and upper secondary education. The training is also available to tutors (1 668 had participated by 2016) and school principals (2 961 had also participated by 2015). Participants reported feeling more confident and secure in their classrooms, and their teaching was more varied and student-centred. In 2017, the total cost of the programme was estimated at EUR 56 million. The evaluation did not take into account the impact of the programme on students' learning outcomes, however. As of 2018, new mathematics modules are available on the Learning Portal, which aim to provide teachers, specialist teachers or specialist support teachers with tools to develop teaching for students with additional needs. During 2018/19, supervisors can take part in a web-based supervisor training to acquire the skills to supervise participant teacher groups (OECD, 2019[1]).

In 2015, The Literacy **Boost** (*Läslyftet*, 2015-20), was launched to provide teachers in Sweden with an in-service training programme in literacy. The programme is also now being offered to preschool teachers as part of a broader effort to strengthen the educational mission of preschools and also to promote the teaching of Swedish at an early age for, among others, children whose mother tongue is not Swedish. The Swedish Government allocated about SEK 50 million per year to The Literacy Boost programme during 2017-19 and about SEK 75 million in 2020. Furthermore, The Literacy Boost has been extended to 2021 (OECD, 2019[1]); (National information reported to the OECD).

Progress or impact: According to the final evaluation from 2020, about 25 percent of all teachers and preschool teachers have participated in the Literacy Boost (Läslyftet). The final evaluation of *Läslyftet* (2020) found that two key goals have been met: developing different teaching methods for language development, and developing a collaborative teaching culture (National information reported to the OECD).

For more information on progress or impact:

Österholm, M. et al. (2016), *Evaluation of the Mathematics Boost: Final Report* (Utvärdering av Matematiklyftets Resultat: Slutrapport), Umeå Mathematics Education Research Centre, Umeå, https://www.skolverket.se/getFile?file=3706.

Wales (United Kingdom): Pioneer Schools Network (2015)

Wales has made a concerted effort in recent years to promote collaborative working and learning across the school system. The establishment of the Pioneer Schools Network (2015) has placed school-to-school collaboration at the core of the design, development and implementation of a new curriculum for Wales. The regional consortia look to nominate schools that exhibit, among other things, excellent leadership, a passion for innovation and creativity and a commitment to professional development as Pioneer Schools. All Pioneer Schools are expected to work with each other, other schools, the consortia, the Welsh government and wider stakeholders as part of an all-Wales partnership. Pioneer Schools meet regularly at the national and regional level, both face-to-face and on line, to share experiences of innovation and learn from one another. The first wave of Pioneer Schools focused on the development of the Digital Competence Framework. Curriculum Pioneers, who looked at content and assessment of learning and New Deal Pioneers, who focused on reforms related to practitioners' professional development, joined these Digital Pioneers from 2016 onwards. The Welsh government brings together quality assurance partners, including HEIs and other experts to review and provide regular feedback to the Pioneer Network (OECD, 2019[1]).

Progress or impact: As of 2018, around 94 primary and secondary schools had been appointed Curriculum Pioneers, 83 as New Deal Pioneers and 13 as Digital Pioneers. In 2017, the OECD found that Pioneer Schools played a pivotal role in driving the development of new curricula and student assessments. Furthermore, a 2018 evaluation found that the Pioneer School model is an innovative approach to reform in Wales, representing a new way of working for all partners and demonstrating a clear commitment to empowering and supporting teachers. This has helped establish an enthusiasm for reform and a clear sense of ownership among Pioneer School representatives. However, this evaluation also emphasises that the complex change management model inevitably means that there are significant risks regarding coherence and consistency. Some of these risks have been mitigated across implementation phases by clarification of expectations, outputs and timescales and the strengthening of monitoring and accountability mechanisms. Finally, Pioneer Schools are obliged to cascade learning and experiences to their assigned Partner Schools. However, the evaluation found that this activity has been relatively limited across the network. New mechanisms are being put in place to address this (OECD, 2019[1]).

For more information on progress or impact:

Arad Research and ICF Consulting (2018), *Formative Evaluation of the Pioneer School Model: Final Report,* Welsh Government, Cardiff, https://dera.ioe.ac.uk/31270/.

Annex 7. Selected current policy efforts to support professional learning

This annex provides further descriptions of current policy initiatives selected for analysis in lesson two. The policies selected are examples of professional learning initiatives that aim to strengthen educators' professional skills and knowledge and that also make use of key policy levers of educator responsiveness and resilience. These policies were developed in response to the new demands placed on educators during the COVID-19 pandemic.

Australia: New Regulatory Strategy for Vocational Education and Training 2020-2022

The Australian Skills Quality Authority (ASQA) has developed a regulatory strategy for 2020-22 based on responses from consultations with stakeholders. The strategy takes a risk-based approach, identifying the system- and provider-level risks to the delivery and quality of VET and taking regulatory action to address the most serious among those identified. As such, this strategy considered the impact of the COVID-19 pandemic on the VET and international education sectors. System-level risks include: providers adding training programmes to meet changes in demand without sufficiently engaging industry experts; providers transitioning to online or other distance modes of delivery without providing adequate student support or the means to validate assessments; and providers being unable to place learners in workplaces to fulfil assessment requirements. To help minimise these risks, ASQA publishes general information and guidance to the sector on related issues and collates further information on a dedicated webpage with advice for providers on how to manage their own risks (e.g. information on distance and online delivery methods, webinars on key risk areas). ASQA also offers targeted advice for individual providers moving to online delivery. Finally, ASQA will also commence a strategic review of online learning in the VET sector. This will engage with key stakeholder groups and providers to understand the benefits, opportunities and risks associated with the transition to online learning during the COVID-19 pandemic, as well as the areas where providers may still face challenges, and where ASQA can provide further support (ASQA, 2020[7]).

Chile: Online Learning for Teachers (Aprendo En Línea Docente) portal

In June, as part of the Learning Recovery Plan, Chile launched an online learning portal for teachers to support them in delivering the new Prioritised School Curriculum, which was prepared by the Ministry of Education (MINEDUC) after the suspension of in-person classes. The portal houses more than 20 000 pedagogical resources, including learning guides, videos, guidelines and assessment tools. Resources are organised by subject and education level. There is also a bank of past and upcoming events and webinars carried out by the Curriculum and Evaluation unit of MINEDUC (MINEDUC, 2020[8]).

Chile: Distance Mentoring (Mentorías a Distancia) for School Management Teams

Normally supporting schools through in-person visits, Chile's Education Quality Agency has adapted its work, developing a programme of remote mentoring for management teams. The Agency conducts three video calls with participants. The first is to identify the main needs in areas such as learning assessment, socio-emotional support, and adapting pedagogical resources. Based on this, the second call discusses and explains specific tools and guidance. Finally, the third call is used to share experiences and analyse results. After the first two months of the programme's implementation, the Education Quality Agency had conducted more than 700 distance mentoring sessions in establishments across the country. Early data suggested that the areas of greatest need among management teams were formative student assessment and socio-emotional support (Education Quality Agency, 2020[9]; Education Quality Agency, 2020[10]).

Colombia: Adaptation of the Let's All Learn (Programa Todos a Aprender) Programme

Within the framework of the Let's all Learn programme (*Programa Todos a Aprender*), Colombia is carrying out online training and guidance for teachers in 4 500 primary level institutions across the country. Programme tutors accompany teachers of mathematics, language and early years education to adapt their practice for distance education, and advise those teachers who need to strengthen their skills. The Ministry of Education has also developed the Contact Teacher platform, through which teachers and school leaders can continue their process of professional and personal training, and share information and teaching experiences (Ministry of Education, Chile, 2020[11]).

France: All Mobilised for Higher Education (SupSolidaire) platform

France's All Mobilised in Higher Education (*SupSolidaire*) campaign seeks to promote initiatives set up in higher education institutions in France both during lockdown and for the new academic year. HEIs submit their initiatives that are then centralised on an interactive map via the Ministry of Higher Education, Research and Innovation's website. The themes covered include: distance learning and working, support for students or staff with disabilities, guidance and professional integration initiatives and support initiatives for teachers in distance education. By sharing knowledge in this way, France aims to disseminate best practice and inspire action at the institutional level (Ministry of Higher Education, 2020[12]).

Ireland: Induction programme, release days for school leaders and extra teaching staff

Ireland is introducing a range of measures to support school leaders and teachers in the new academic year. Prior to schools reopening, all staff must complete COVID-19 Induction Training that will ensure that staff have full knowledge of the latest public health advice and guidance and an outline of the COVID-19 response plan. The Professional Development Service for Teachers has developed an interactive resource bank for teachers to support teaching, learning and assessment. Moreover, at primary level, Ireland is providing funding to allow school leaders and some deputy school leaders who also have teaching hours to have one release day per week during the next academic year. At secondary level, 1 080 additional teaching posts, including 120 guidance posts, have been introduced to support schools in managing the extra workload resulting from efforts to minimise the impact of the COVID-19 pandemic (Department of Education and Skills, Ireland, 2020[13]).

Ireland: Reflecting and learning through stakeholder consultation in higher education

Ireland's National Forum for the Enhancement of Teaching and Learning in Higher Education, the national body responsible for strengthening teaching and learning in higher education, carried out a comprehensive feedback exercise to help inform the new academic year 2020/21. In order to identify key lessons from the period of institutional closures, the National Forum approached key contacts across the sector with one question: What do you know now with respect to teaching and learning that you wish you had known before this all began? The National Forum received individual and collective responses from 28 higher education institutions, as well as from the Union of Students in Ireland and the National Student Engagement Programme. These responses took various forms, including extensive written documents, brief reflective paragraphs, recorded conversations, bullet lists and collated responses from colleagues across an institution. In June, the National Forum published a report, *Reflecting and Learning: the Move to Remote/Online Teaching And Learning in Irish Higher Education*, summarising the key insights and contextualising them within international and national evidence on the enhancement of teaching and learning. The report also identified key practices and outlooks to maintain when planning the new semester, and the challenges that require attention if the increase in online/remote teaching and learning is to be sustained, even partially, over the longer term (National Forum for the Enhancement of Teaching and Learning in Higher Education, 2020[14]).

Korea: National online teacher community and Knowledge Spring (지식샘터)

Korea established an online community of 10 000 representative teachers, one from almost every school across the country, to promote the exchange of good practice in online education, and to give advice to help address any issues colleagues encounter. The community provides a real-time, interactive communications channel among 17 Provincial Offices of Education, the 10 000 representative teachers nationwide and other relevant institutions, including the Ministry of Education. As well as supporting teachers during the crisis, the community has a longer-term function: based on successful outcomes of this initiative, the Ministry of Education will continue the support for a cohort of educational innovators, who will become the driving force behind artificial intelligence and future-driven education (Ministry of Education, Korea, 2020[15]).

Alongside the online community, Korea has also launched the Knowledge Spring online platform for teachers, an autonomous and personalised remote teacher training system. Teachers and instructors can flexibly organise and operate teaching materials, content and training time to suit their identified needs. This differs from the existing institutional-led training models that may be less individualised (MOE, 2020[16]).

Turkey: Distance Education Centres (Uzaktan Eğitim Merkezi) established in public higher education institutions

For the academic year 2020/21, Turkey is promoting distance and blended learning approaches in higher education. New regulations enable HEIs to deliver 40% of all formal programmes offered through distance education while also introducing the expectation that at least 10% of all formal programmes will be delivered through distance education. To support institutions in capitalising on these new regulations, public universities will be assigned additional staff and research assistants to work in new or existing Distance Education Centres. Following the establishment of 20 new Distance Education Centres, every public university in the country now has one; the government also recently passed a recommendation to establish these Centres in all foundation universities. These Centres support institutional practices for distance education and conduct related research. The Higher Education Council is also implementing a training programme to raise the competencies of staff in these Centres (Higher Education Council, Turkey, 2020[17]).

Annex 8. Recent work from the OECD's Teachers' Professional Learning Study

The OECD's Teachers' Professional Learning (TPL) Study aims to help countries develop efficient, equitable and sustainable teacher learning systems at both system and school level. The project covers the full cycle of professional learning, from initial education and induction to continuing professional learning, and works with volunteer countries to build resilient TPL systems, with a strong focus on peer learning.

Ensuring the continuity, timeliness and relevance of teachers' professional learning has been a priority for many countries during the COVID-19 disruption of schooling. This box provides an insight into a key finding of the project during the COVID-19 crisis. It offers further substantive background to the Education Policy Reform Dialogues 2020, Session 2 – *Schools (general instruction and VET): Strengthening professional learning for educators and closing learning gaps in an academic year of more flexible schooling.*

Box 5. Insights from the TPL Study on professional learning during the COVID-19 pandemic

Among other priorities, the crisis created an urgent need for professional learning related to remote teaching and distance learning. It also accelerated the use of technology in TPL. In this context, innovative and teacher-led initiatives, such as online professional learning communities, have received renewed attention. At the same time, the economic crisis related to the pandemic has created new budgetary pressures, and professional development risks being an area of investment that may suffer. In response to the COVID-19 crisis, the TPL Study has adapted the methodology for its country diagnosis strand. The TPL Study identifies teacher leadership and collaboration in professional learning as key levers. For the current academic term, fostering a culture of professional trust and ensuring the continuity of teachers' access to professional learning through online platforms will be key to supporting such collaboration. Research evidence has emphasised the importance of peer observation and collaborative learning communities for enhancing teaching practices but also the limited opportunities teachers have for collaboration. To support engagement in collaborative learning, effective school leadership and facilitation (e.g. making time for collaboration in teachers' schedules) can help develop a professional culture of trust. Digital technologies further expand the scope for collaborative practices and help overcome geographic, physical or financial constraints. When well-designed and moderated, online learning communities can enhance supportive professional practices and valuable professional learning.

The **Flemish Community of Belgium** is among the first education systems participating in a country diagnosis with the TPL study. *KlasCement* (1998), an educational resources network managed by the Flemish Department of Education and Training, illustrates the role online communities can play. Created as a "community for and by teachers", *KlasCement* targets teachers at all education levels who can share their own resources, search for inspiring resources from other teachers or organisations, and exchange with each other through a teacher forum. In the context of the pandemic, *KlasCement* has increased its efforts by curating existing resources, organising webinars on relevant topics for remote learning and redesigning the teacher forum to enable more effective teacher discussions.

Since its launch, a key feature of implementation has been building a culture of trust: the network started as a bottom-up initiative, managed by a team of teachers who monitor and publish educational resources submitted by users. During COVID-19, challenges have mostly revolved around communication and ICT (Information and communication technology) infrastructure (e.g. capacity and privacy-related concerns). In this respect, the development of *KlasCement* has shown that a number of factors are key for successful implementation of such a network: involving teachers' at all stages to build trust and develop a sense of agency, investing in high-quality ICT infrastructure, and relying on a network support team composed of teachers.

Sources: Boeskens, Nusche and Yurita (2020[18]), "Policies to support teachers' continuing professional learning: A conceptual framework and mapping of OECD data", *OECD Education Working Papers*, OECD Publishing, Paris; OECD (2019[19]), *OECD Teachers' Professional Learning (TPL) Study Design and Implementation Plan*, http://www.oecd.org/education/school-resources-review/TPL-Study-Design-and-Implementation-Plan.pdf; Mineea-Pic (forthcoming[20]), "Flemish Community of Belgium: KlasCement", *Education Continuity Stories Series*, OECD Publishing, Paris.

For more information please visit: http://www.oecd.org/education/teachers-professional-learning-study/.

Annex 9. Policies addressing learning gaps from the pre-crisis period with evidence of positive impact

This annex provides further descriptions and evaluative findings for the policies from the pre-crisis period that were selected for analysis in lesson three. The information comes from previously published material from the Education Policy Outlook, which was drafted in consultation with participating education systems. The policies selected focus on recovering and mitigating learning gaps, show evidence of having made positive progress towards policy objectives, and make use of key policy levers of learner and system resilience and responsiveness.

Australia: The National Indigenous Reform Agreement (2007)

Since 2007, the National Indigenous Reform Agreement, also known as Closing the Gap, in Queensland has aimed to increase the number of Aboriginal and Torres Strait Islander students achieving Year 12 Certification. Measures were taken at the central, regional and local level. For example, in the state of Queensland, the central office's Department of Education provided each region with disaggregated data to quantify increases in certification for which they should aim. This helped regions to visualise the objectives. Other measures included raising awareness of the importance of change among school leaders and regional staff, through workshops and leadership sessions. In addition, Queensland's educational regions provided support to schools (for example, by appointing coaches for the Queensland Certificate of Education), and schools set up multi-disciplinary case-management teams to aid students (OECD, 2018[21]).

Progress or impact: The government reports that between 2006 and 2015, the proportion of Indigenous 20-24 year-olds with Year 12 or equivalent attainment increased from 45.4% to 61.5%. Improvements were also identified in the retention rate of Aboriginal and Torres Strait Islander students in high school in Queensland. In 2015, almost 60% of Indigenous students stayed in school until Year 12. Improvements were also identified for preschool enrolment, which had increased to 87% for Aboriginal and Torres Strait Islander children by 2015. The number of Indigenous students with a Year 12 Certification increased from 42.1% in 2008 to 97% by 2016. The success of the programme to reduce the gap can be attributed to the alignment across schools, regional offices and central office; a clear line of sight to individual schools and students; and intensive case management (OECD, 2018[21]).

For more information on progress or impact:

Commonwealth of Australia, Department of the Prime Minister and Cabinet (2019), *Closing the Gap Report 2019*, Australian Government, Canberra, https://antar.org.au/sites/default/files/2019_ctg_report.pdf.

Australia: The Higher Education Participation and Partnerships Programme (2010)

In Australia, the Higher Education Participation and Partnerships Programme (HEPPP) aims to ensure that Australians from low socio-economic backgrounds who have the ability to study at university have the opportunity to do so. Through its Participation and Partnerships components, HEPPP provides funding to assist universities to undertake activities and implement strategies that improve access to undergraduate courses for people from low socio-economic backgrounds, as well as improving the retention and completion rates of those students. Partnerships are created with primary and secondary schools, VET institutions, universities and other stakeholders to raise the aspirations and build the capacity of disadvantaged students to participate in higher education. Funding for these two components is provided to universities based on the number of enrolled students from low socio-economic backgrounds. The third component, the National Priorities Pool, funds projects that target and support building an evidence base for future equity policies, testing new equity interventions at the national and institutional levels, and improving implementation of HEPPP at these levels (OECD, 2018[21]).

Progress or impact: A 2016 evaluation found that HEPPP is positively influencing the quantity and rigour of higher education equity activities and policies overall. It concluded that HEPPP has provided wide-ranging support to a large number of students and institutions between 2010 and 2015. Some 2 679 projects were implemented at the 37 eligible universities. Over 310 000 students have participated in HEPPP projects, with additional students supported in schools and other institutions. At least 2 913 partner organisations participated in HEPPP outreach activities (OECD, 2018[21]).

For more information on progress or impact:

ACIL Allen Consulting (2017), *Evaluation of the Higher Education Participation and Partnerships Programmes*, Report to the Department of Education and Training, Melbourne, https://docs.education.gov.au/system/files/doc/other/final_heppp_evaluation_report_2017.03.16_0.pdf.

Department of Education, Skills and Employment 2020, '*Higher Education Participation and Partnership Program*', Commonwealth of Australia, https://www.education.gov.au/higher-education-participation-and-partnerships-programme-heppp.

Nova Scotia (Canada): The Schools Plus Programme (2008)

The Schools Plus programme, launched in 2008 in the province of Nova Scotia, is an interagency approach to support children and families by appointing the school as the centre of service delivery. The programme's core focus continues to be the creation of "communities of care" to help students foster resilience and prevent more children, youth and families from becoming at risk. Ultimately, the programme aims to reach and support the 5-10% of children and youth in Nova Scotia who are at risk of marginalisation. The policy has expanded every year, with sites in all eight education entities (formerly school boards). Each education entity now has a Schools Plus facilitator and Community Outreach Workers who act as the liaison between the school and the community, and each education entity has established a Schools Plus Advisory Committee, which identifies opportunities to enhance and expand the array of services and programmes for children, youth and their families (OECD, 2018[21]).

Progress or impact: A 2013 report highlighted that the Schools Plus programme had achieved provincial coverage, after establishing 95 sites in all eight school education entities. Although the service provided by the programme had resulted in an increase in interdepartmental service co-operation and the introduction of mental health services, the report suggested that a "mid-term correction" should be made to ensure that the policy achieves its ultimate goal. However, the report states that the programme has been more successful at "co-ordinating existing public social services" than achieving its original mission (OECD, 2018[21]).

For more information on progress or impact:

Crinean, K. et al. (2012), *Evaluation of Schools Plus – Year Three Final Report*, Collective Wisdom Solutions, Halifax, https://www.ednet.ns.ca/schoolsplus/en/files-schoolsplus/sp_evaluation-year3-final-september24.pdf.

Chile: Preferential School Subsidy (2008)

Through the Preferential School Subsidy (*Ley de Subvención Escolar Preferencial*, SEP) in Chile, primary schools receive additional funding for enrolment of socio-economically disadvantaged students. These funds are in addition to the baseline funding that public and government-subsidised private schools receive for each enrolled student. In 2008, the introduction of the preferential education subsidy modified this scheme to make it more equity-oriented. It allocates a large share of expenditure on a per-student basis (topping up the flat-rate voucher) and provides an additional amount for schools that enrol a significant proportion of students from low socio-economic backgrounds. Acceptance of these funds is voluntary. Concretely, schools that receive the supplement have to sign an agreement, elaborate a plan for education improvement, set objectives and define measures to support students with learning difficulties. Schools are categorised as autonomous, emerging or recovering, based on criteria such as their results in the national standardised assessment of student performance (*Sistema de Medición de Calidad de la Educación*). Depending on their category, schools either design their own educational improvement plan, receive support from the Education Ministry to draft their progress plans or get external technical assistance. Struggling schools that fail to improve after receiving assistance risk losing their licence or their eligibility for the subsidy (OECD, 2018[21]).

Progress or impact: SEP resulted in important changes in the Chilean school system. Although the programme is voluntary, around 85% of the 9 000 eligible schools participated in 2011. All municipal schools and about 66% of private subsidised schools are actively engaged. This high coverage has changed the relationship between schools and the Ministry of Education and has helped improve its regressive funding structure. Although some schools were reticent to accept the conditions imposed by the agreement, most schools have welcomed the new resources, as well as the clear pedagogical goals and diagnostic tools tailored to help meet them. Studies show positive effects on student performance. In 2015, SEP served 94% of all municipal schools (including 99% of those providing basic education) and 50% of private subsidised schools (including 75% of those providing basic education). It is not possible to convincingly estimate the effects on student learning in public schools, since participation in SEP is almost universal. However, research has found some positive effects of SEP on private subsidised schools, such as an increase in standardised student assessment scores on average and larger increases for schools with more significant enrolment of low-income students. In recent years, the SEP Law increased its resources by 20% for the education of the most vulnerable students of the system (defined as "priority students"). In addition, the preferential school subsidy was created for "preferential students". Schools that are in SEP and do not charge a co-payment receive it for each student who belongs to the poorest 80% of the country and is not "priority" (OECD, 2018[21]).

For more information on progress or impact:

Irarrázaval, I. et al (2012), *Evaluation of the first years of Implementation of the Preferential School Subsidy* (Evaluación de los primeros años de Implementación del Programa de Subvención Escolar Preferencial, de la Subsecretaría de Educación), Centre for Public Policy, Pontifical Catholic University of Chile, Santiago, https://www.researchgate.net/publication/320735176_Evaluacion_de_los_primeros_anos_de_Implementacion_del_Programa_de_Subvencion_Escolar_Preferencial_de_la_Subsecretaria_de_Educacion?enrichId=rgreq-7866d6507a522842331bcfed8e20ebf8-XXX&enrichSource=Y292ZXJQYWdlOzMyMDczNTE3NjtBUzo1NTU4OTM2NDExODMyMzJAMTUwOTU0Njc4MDEwOA%3D%3D&el=1_x_2&_esc=publicationCoverPdf.

Estonia: Pathfinder Centres (2015)

A network of Pathfinder (*Rajaleidja*, 2015) centres, co-ordinated by the Innove Foundation, provide educational counselling services to parents, teachers, and other adults working with young people between the ages of 1.5 and 18. Pathfinder centres identify the young people's learning and behavioural needs, and direct them towards additional support from specialists such as psychologists or speech therapists. During recent school closures, the Pathfinder centres continued to provide remote counselling and support to schools and families (OECD, 2020[22]).

For more information on progress or impact:

CIVITTA (2017), *Mid-term Evaluation of the Study and Career Guidance Programme: Final Report* (Õppe-ja Karjäärinõustamise Programmi Vahehindamine: Lõpparuanne), CIVITTA – The Challenge Advisory, Tartu, https://www.hm.ee/sites/default/files/aruanne_1.pdf.

Finland: Preparatory Curricula for immigrant students (2009, updated 2015)

In 2015, Finland implemented the National Core Curriculum for Instruction Preparing for Basic Education, to respond to the need to better integrate immigrant students. It outlines key strategic areas in education, including securing equal opportunity in education and culture and promoting participation and inclusion. At least 32 500 refugees arrived in Finland in 2015. By the end of that year, almost 3 500 students were attending preparatory courses for basic education. To respond to the needs of this new refugee population, the government established 50 new groups of preparatory studies for basic education in municipalities. In 2015, at least 200 immigrant students were preparing for upper secondary education. Students have access to courses in either Finnish or Swedish, or they can attend classes in their native language. Students age 6-10 receive at least 900 hours of instruction, and older students are eligible to receive at least 1 000 hours. However, no national syllabus has been designed for the curriculum. Students who are able to keep up with the instruction are eligible to transfer to basic education regardless of whether they have completed the required hours. In 2015, the government also implemented the National Core Curriculum for Instruction Preparing for Basic Education, the National Core Curriculum for Instruction Preparing for General Upper Secondary Education, and Preparatory Education for Vocational Training. These three policies include measures for students from immigrant backgrounds originally included in the National Core Curriculum for Instruction Preparing Immigrants for Basic Education (2009), which has been discontinued (OECD, 2018[21]).

Progress or impact: As of 2016, around 12% of immigrant students had classes in Finnish or Swedish as a second language, while 25% did not have separate language classes. The 2016 report by the working group of the Ministry of Education and Culture on immigrant issues states that it is important to their language development to grant separate Finnish or Swedish language classes as well as to aid the development of immigrant students' mother tongues. In fact, in 2014, more than 16 000 students participated in courses taught in their own mother language, resulting in a total of 53 different languages being taught (OECD, 2018[21]).

Updated information: To strengthen the integration of immigrants, a revised National Core Curriculum for Preparatory Instruction in Basic Education (2015), emphasising Finnish or Swedish as a second language and mother-tongue instruction for other subjects, was introduced. Students receive up to 1 000 hours' instruction (900 hours maximum for 6-10 year-olds); transition to mainstream education occurs flexibly. Preparatory studies also exist for general upper secondary, VET, and adult basic education. According to a report from the Ministry of Education and Culture (2016), by late 2015, around one-third of young migrants arriving in 2014/15 attended such programmes. An evaluation (2018) found the programme inclusive and integrative, but quality varied by teachers' skills or attitudes. The OECD (2018) also called for greater consistency across municipalities (OECD, 2020[3]).

For more information on progress or impact:

OECD (2018), Working Together: Skills and Labour Market Integration of Immigrants and their Children in Finland, OECD Publishing, Paris, https://doi.org/10.1787/9789264305250-en.

Ministry of Education and Culture, Finland (2016), *The Educational Tracks and Integration of Immigrants – Problematic Areas and Proposals for Actions*, Publications of the OKM, Helsinki, https://julkaisut.valtioneuvosto.fi/bitstream/handle/10024/64986/okm6.pdf?sequence=1&isAllowed=y.

Finland: Student Welfare Act (2013)

Finland's Student Welfare Act (2013) guarantees students access to services including psychologists, social workers and healthcare. Taking a preventative approach, it promotes well-being at schools and individualised support built on collaboration between professionals, students and families. A 2018 evaluation concluded that a more systematic, multi-disciplinary approach has been implemented, but with inconsistencies across providers. The OECD (2019) reported that the share of students in compulsory education receiving support doubled to 17.5% between 2013 and 2017. Finland maintained these services during school closures for the COVID-19 pandemic (OECD, 2020[3]).

For more information on progress or impact:

FINEEC (2018), "Extensive evaluation: pupil and student welfare has been enhanced after the enforcement of the Pupil and Student Welfare Act, but the development work is far from over", *FINEEC – News*, FINEEC, webpage, https://karvi.fi/en/2018/03/14/extensive-evaluation-pupil-student-welfare-enhanced-enforcementpupil-student-welfare-act-development-work-far/ (accessed 02 October 2020).

Germany: Education Alliances (2013)

Since 2013, Education Alliances (*Kultur macht stark – Bündnisse für Bildung*) have supported out-of-school programmes in Germany for educationally disadvantaged children and teenagers. Starting in 2013, the Federal Ministry of Education and Research (*Bundesministerium für Bildung und Forschung*, BMBF) allocated annual funding of EUR 30 million for this programme, to be increased to EUR 50 million in the following four years. The Education Package (*Bildungspaket*) (by the Federal Ministry of Labour and Social Affairs, 2011) aims to give 2.5 million children from disadvantaged backgrounds the opportunity to participate in activities such as school excursions, sports, and musical and cultural activities, to boost their motivation and sense of belonging (OECD, 2018[21]).

Progress or impact: A 2016 evaluation found overall positive results for the policy. By 2016, 11 500 measures had been taken, and 4 700 alliances had been funded across the country. The main target group of educationally disadvantaged children and teenagers benefitted from at least 90% of the measures taken. Between 2013 and 2016, 223 000 children and teenagers as well as 28 000 relatives benefitted from out-of school programmes. The main geographical focus is on regions with a high percentage of the main target group. Success factors identified include easy access to the programmes for children and teenagers, as well as content tailored to conditions on the ground. Other factors are the possibility to gain social and cultural awareness and skills: 90% of the alliances include volunteers. An important target is also the establishment of long-term co-operation. Of the co-ordinators interviewed, 65% stated they intended to reapply for funding. In addition, 90% of the alliances anticipated continuing the co-operation independently of the federal programme. The programme will be extended from 2018 to 2022, and interested local partners can begin applying for 2018 funding at the end of 2017 (OECD, 2018[21]).

For more information on progress or impact:

Prognos (2016), *Culture Makes you Strong: Education Alliances Report on the Evaluation Period 2014-2015 (*Kultur macht stark: Bündnisse für Bildung: Bericht zum Evaluationszeitraum 2014-2015, BMBF, Freiburg/Düsseldorf, https://www.prognos.com/publikationen/alle-publikationen/657/show/78f89294c67ee434a07bc2dc0dee73d0/.

Ireland: Delivering Equality of Opportunity in Schools (2005, 2017)

The Delivering Equality of Opportunity in Schools (DEIS) Plan 2017 has been the main policy initiative tackling educational disadvantage. It builds on the DEIS Plan for Educational Inclusion (2005), which provided a range of targeted support to the most disadvantaged schools. From 2017, 79 schools were added and 30 received enhanced support, including programmes targeting transition, well-beingwellbeing and teachers' professional development. New targets were also introduced for student retention and progression, as well as initiatives to improve adult and family literacy. The Educational Research Centre (2017; 2018) found that achievement and attainment gaps between DEIS and non-DEIS schools have generally narrowed at both primary and post-primary levels, but remain significant. In the same way, student retention, literacy and, to a lesser extent, numeracy, have improved (OECD, 2020[5]).

For more information on progress or impact:

Weir, S. and L. Kavanagh (2018), *The Evaluation of DEIS at Post-Primary Level: Closing the Achievement and Attainment Gaps*, Dublin, Educational Research Centre, http://www.erc.ie/wp-content/uploads/2019/01/Weir-Kavanagh-2018-DEIS-post-primary.pdf.

Kavanagh, L., S. Weir and E. Moran (2017), The Evaluation of DEIS: Monitoring Achievement and Attitudes among Urban Primary School Pupils from 2007 to 2016, Educational Research Centre, Dublin, http://www.erc.ie/wp-content/uploads/2017/06/DEIS-report-2017.pdf.

Norway: Certificate of Practice Scheme (2008, 2011)

The Certificate of Practice Scheme (*Praksisbrev*) is an alternative VET pathway aimed at students who are struggling in mainstream VET. Its aim is to improve completion rates among these students. The scheme was piloted between 2008 and 2011 and was adopted as a permanent arrangement in 2016. Whereas most VET programmes in Norway involve two years of school-based learning before beginning a two-year apprenticeship period, certificate of practice candidates alternate between school-based training and training in enterprise. At the end of the programme, students can transition to the journeyman's certificate (a formal VET qualification) or continue their training in a particular trade. An evaluation by the Norwegian Research Institute (NIFU) found that 49% of Certificate of Practice students obtained an apprenticeship after completing the programme, compared to 29% of students in mainstream VET. The evaluation linked the success of the programme to the degree of work-based learning, which was a better fit for some learners than school-based learning. Giving students the opportunity to establish contact with enterprises early in the programme also meant that these students were more likely to secure an apprenticeship with the same employer (OECD, 2020[23]).

For more information on progress or impact:

European Centre for the Development of Vocational Training (n.d.), *Certificate of Practice (Praksisbrev)*, CEDEFOP, Thessaloniki, https://www.cedefop.europa.eu/en/printpdf/toolkits/vet-toolkit-tackling-early-leaving/resources/certificate-practice-praksisbrev (accessed on 02 October 2020).

Portugal: National Programme to Promote Educational Success (2016)

Portugal has introduced a comprehensive national strategy with a focus on combating school failure and grade repetition, the National Programme to Promote Educational Success (*Plano Nacional de Promoção do Sucesso Escolar*, PNPSE). The Plan takes a preventative approach, promoting academic success and the improvement of learning, particularly in the early years of schooling. It supports schools to develop improvement plans, based on the principle that educational communities best understand their contexts, difficulties and capabilities and are better prepared to design plans for strategic action. The Plan also aims to examine individual students' competences more comprehensively across a range of disciplines, including the introduction of a basic student profile, and to support students who have already repeated grades through additional tutoring. School autonomy is also reinforced, especially on pedagogic issues, through the Curriculum Flexibility and Autonomy programme (OECD, 2018[21]).

Progress or impact: The coverage of the PNPSE is high, with 663 schools developing a strategic plan around the framework for their schools. The PNPSE, combined with the schools that are already participating in similar activities through the Third Generation of the Education Territories of Priority

Intervention Programme (TEIP3), now covers almost 99% of Portugal's 811 schools. According to a recent European Commission report, the success of the plan in raising performance will depend on capacity to provide technical support and ensure regular monitoring of actions and overall coherence of the different projects (OECD, 2018[21]).

Updated information: The National Programme to Promote Educational Success (*Programa Nacional de Promoção do Sucesso Escolar*, PNPSE, 2016) is a comprehensive strategy to combat school failure and grade repetition. PNPSE takes a preventative approach, promoting academic success in the first cycle of primary education via enhanced classroom interactions, early-intervention, teacher collaboration and comprehensive evaluation of student competences. There has been strong emphasis on building capacity for teachers and school leaders; PNPSE supports schools to develop improvement plans for their context and by 2018, 663 schools had done so. PNPSE also supports municipalities to develop local projects aligned with school actions; by 2018, 2 915 different actions had been defined locally, then disseminated nationally. However, the European Commission found that ensuring technical support, ongoing monitoring and overall coherence remain challenges (OECD, 2020[6]).

For more information on progress or impact:

Verdasca, J., (n.d.), *National Programme for the Promotion of School Success: Presentation Note,* Website of the PNPSE, Ministry of Education, Portugal, https://pnpse.min-educ.pt/programa (accessed on 02 October 2020).

Slovenia: Project for the Successful Integration of Roma Students in Schools (2008-15)

In 2008, the Ministry of Education, Science and Sports in Slovenia, with the help of the European Structural Funds, implemented the Project for the Successful Integration of Roma Students in Schools (2008-15). It aimed to share national best practices of inclusive teaching among kindergartens and schools and teachers in areas with little or no such experience. One of the most important measures was providing a Roma assistant in Roma settlements and schools attended by Roma pupils. Following promising results of this policy, the government later implemented a series of projects to expand support to Roma communities. The project on Raising the Social and Cultural Capital in Areas Inhabited by Members of the Roma Community (2011-13) aimed to work with Roma children, youth and parents in Roma settlements to increase the participation and success of Roma children in education. More recently, the Together for Knowledge (2016-21) programme aims to supply educational support in preschools for Roma communities through the inclusion of Roma parents in educational activities, as well as coaching sessions and after-school activities for children (OECD, 2018[21]).

Progress or impact: The Project for the Successful Integration of Roma Students in Schools was identified by the Council of Europe as a demonstrated good practice (observing the Municipality of Murska Sobota). As reported by the Roma Union, results achieved by the end of 2010 included higher attendance of Roma children in educational institutions, improved co-operation between Roma parents and educational institutions, increased awareness among Roma of the importance of learning and education, and more successful co-operation between teaching assistants, teachers and Roma parents in the education of Roma children. The Council of Europe also identified the importance of the project on Raising the Social and Cultural Capital in Areas Inhabited by Members of the Roma Community (2011-13), particularly its contributions to the design of innovative and creative educational practices in Roma communities (OECD, 2018[21]).

For more information on progress or impact:

Council of Europe (2017), *Fourth Report Submitted by Slovenia Pursuant to Article 25, Paragraph 2 of the Framework Convention for the Protection of National Minorities*, National Minorities (FCNM), Council of Europe, Strasbourg, https://rm.coe.int/16806d3fbc.

Annex 10. Selected current policy efforts to address learning gaps

This annex provides further descriptions of current policy initiatives selected for analysis in lesson three. The policies selected are examples of initiatives to recover and mitigate learning gaps and also make use of key policy levers for learner and system resilience and responsiveness. These policies were developed in response to the challenges facing learners and education systems during the COVID-19 pandemic.

Chile: Tutors for Chile (Tutores para Chile)

Chile's Tutors for Chile (*Tutores para Chile*) network brings together participants of initial teacher education to facilitate tutorials for school students that support schools and teachers in the provision of distance learning. The nature of these tutorials is determined by the host school, in liaison with the teacher training institution and the trainee teacher. Tutorials may be carried out online or in person (once schools reopen) but a supervisor must be present to monitor the work, and give a final evaluation. The tutorials will cover a period of three to four months and will focus on critical levels in education, such as final-year or transition-year students. They will last one hour and take place weekly with one tutor supporting up to three students. In this way, tutors will support the work of schools in helping students overcome learning gaps created or exacerbated by the COVID-19 crisis. At the same time, the tutors are able to continue their own training, gaining the practical experience and professional guidance required for qualification (MINEDUC, 2020[24]).

Chile: Comprehensive Assessment of Learning (Diagnóstico Integral de Aprendizajes) and curricular prioritisation

Chile has introduced a Curricular Prioritisation support package for schools to identify the educational objectives considered essential for learning. The resources support schools in balancing the various curricular areas, ensure coherence and progression across the school year, and provide the skills and knowledge necessary for successful transition to the next school year. The tools cover all levels of schooling and all subjects with an additional differentiated plan for vocational training. Curricular Prioritisation is based on the three basic principles of security, flexibility, and fairness, and will last two years (2020 and 2021), allowing for a gradual transition towards the current general curriculum. These two years are considered as spaces for the recovery and consolidation of essential learning, with flexible criteria on the curriculum and assessment. To support schools and teachers, the Ministry held a virtual conference about curricular prioritisation and, from June, made online training available, with a focus on practice within the classroom and teacher well-being. Other supporting resources include teaching guidelines for the prioritised objectives, with accompanying teaching strategies, resources or students, formative evaluations, videos and digital platforms aligned to the Curricular Prioritisation. The process is not mandatory, and schools have the autonomy to adapt the process to their own context. To facilitate this flexible approach, the government has introduced amendments to legislation (MINEDUC, 2020[25]).

To support schools in the reopening process, Chile's Education Quality Agency developed the Comprehensive Assessment of Learning (DIA). This assesses students' socio-emotional state and their learning in areas such as reading and mathematics, helping schools to identify the gaps that may have resulted from emergency distance education. Schools that resume in-person teaching must register on the DIA platform. The tool is flexible, with schools able to administer the assessments when they want and receive result reports immediately. The platform offers three types of assessment tools: those collecting information on the socio-emotional well-being of students and some socio-emotional skills essential to face this period of crisis; for younger students, an Interactive Diagnosis which generates evidence through participation in the activity; and for older students, short self-report questionnaires which generate a report at the course level. The latter comes with guidance for a follow-up workshop. The Education Quality Agency also provides video mentoring to management teams to support with implementation. The Agency will carry out a sample evaluation at the end of 2020 to determine the status of student learning and the impact of the pandemic (MINEDUC, 2020[26]; MINEDUC, 2020[27]).

France: National benchmarking assessments (tests de positionnement) and additional resources

To support schools in diagnosing learning needs on the return to in-person education, France is directing schools towards several methods. National benchmarking tests, in place since 2017 for students in the first two years of primary education, will take place in September, with a follow-up mid-term assessment in January 2021. National assessments in mathematics and French for students in the first year of lower secondary education will also take place in September, having been further developed to better identify students' needs and offer results that are more useful. These students will also take a new reading fluency test in their first days back at school. France has simplified the procedure for French and mathematics placement tests for students in upper secondary school this year, and introduced new literacy and numeracy tests for those in the first years of the professional vocational education track (CAP). For students in all other levels, teachers will use new short and one-off tests to instantly measure the mastery of fundamental skills and identify priorities for each student. France has identified priority educational objectives for French and mathematics at every level of education. These are accompanied by resources for teachers and must be the focus of teaching and learning during the first weeks of the school year (Ministère de l"Éducation Nationale et de la Jeunesse et des Sports, 2020[28]; Eduscol, 2020[29]).

To support schools in redressing learning gaps, the Ministry is mobilising other additional resources. France is increasing the hours of support available in the first months of the school year through the educational assistants (*assistants d'éducation*) and through the Homework Done (*Devoirs Faits*) initiative, which offers students personalised support and homework help, respectively. Following the health crisis, the government has doubled its previous commitment and is creating 8 000 new support posts for students with disabilities (*accompagnement d'élèves en situation handicap*). There will also be an additional 1 248 new teaching posts in primary education as a direct result of the health crisis (Eduscol, 2020[29]).

Japan: Reinforcing human resources in schools

Japan committed considerable extra resources to support the reopening of schools after the initial lockdown measures. Firstly, the Ministry of Education, Culture, Sports, Science and Technology (MEXT) reinforced human resources for schools that were dividing classes for staggered attendance. Additional teachers enabled multiple smaller classes to run among students in the final years of primary and lower secondary education in order to allow them to receive a sufficient amount of in-person teaching. Between one and three extra instructors were employed per school to assist classroom teachers and, in regions with a high infection rate, school support staff were assigned to schools to support lesson planning, parental contact and COVID-19 related administrative tasks. Finally, school counsellors and social workers were assigned on a school-by-school basis. Japan recruited these extra staff from the pool of retired teachers, tutors, university students and other education-related staff or actors in the community. To facilitate the process, Japan eased qualification requirements for instructors, recognising temporary, special licenses (MEXT, 2020[30]).

The Netherlands: Catch-up Programme (Inhaal en ondersteuningsprogramma's) for the academic year 2020/21

The Netherlands is investing almost an additional EUR 500 million in education in response to the COVID-19 pandemic. Of this amount, EUR 244 million will fund a subsidy scheme for primary and secondary general education, and secondary VET to provide extra support to students. Schools can apply for subsidies to run voluntary catch-up programmes between summer 2020 and 2021. These may take the form of after-school programmes, catch-up programmes during school holidays or extra support during the school day. Students from teacher training courses and pedagogical studies can assist teachers in delivering these interventions. The Ministry provides schools with research summaries to support programme design, as well as concrete proposals as to how to select students, prioritise learning goals and monitor students' progress. Eligible students include: those with learning gaps caused by school closures; those who have experienced delays in their studies or practical training as a result of COVID-19; and those who do not speak Dutch in the home and may need language support. A further EUR 3.8 million has been allocated for the new school year to provide digital equipment to students forced to study at home who do not have a laptop or tablet. All students in VET and higher education programmes who, unable to graduate in 2019/20 due to institutional closures, and who need to re-enrol and graduate in the next academic year will receive funding for approximately three months of tuition fees (Ministry of Education, 2020[31]).

Portugal: School Action Plans for the Recovery and Consolidation of Learning (Plano de Atuação para a recuperação / consolidação das aprendizagens)

Portugal has directed schools to focus the first five weeks of the new school year on learning recovery. All schools must develop an Action Plan for the Recovery and Consolidation of Learning that guides teaching and learning throughout the year, intensively so in the first weeks, and should be flexible enough to withstand possible future closures. To support schools, the government has produced a set of guidelines for the organisation of the school year, along with a comprehensive roadmap for recovery and consolidation, which includes example activities and learning tools and approaches for schools. Specific support measures include an increase in hourly credits – the time allocated to schools for non-teaching related activities including management, student pastoral care and personalised learning, as well as teacher planning and collaboration – for the academic year 2020/21. The extra time must be used exclusively for activities related to learning recovery and consolidation. Portugal has also extended the Specific tutorial support programme- originally reserved for students in secondary education who have repeated a year twice- to all students who did not pass the school year in 2019/20. All schools must also establish a peer mentoring programme in which volunteer mentors from the student body are paired with student mentees (Ministry of Education, Portugal, 2020[32]).

The work of the latter two schemes is overseen by the school's pedagogical council. Portugal encourages all schools to carry out assessments to identify all students' needs to enable a more personalised approach to learning recovery. Schools should begin with an assessment of students' digital skills and the digital resources available to them, then use curricular documents and essential learning objectives to map where the students' gaps in learning are. Through this, school teams should determine individualised learning paths for students. The process should involve students as much as possible. Schools should take advantage of an increase in support offered by the multi-disciplinary inclusion support teams. Portugal also committed EUR 125 million euros for extra human resources in educational institutions. This will cover new teaching posts, as well as additional positions for non-teaching staff, and 800 specialists such as social workers and psychologists (Ministry of Education, Portugal, 2020[32]).

England (United Kingdom): Catch-Up Premium

In England, the government has committed GBP 1 billion to fund educational catch-up initiatives. This includes a one-off, universal catch-up premium for the 2020-2021 academic year which provides primary and lower-secondary schools with an extra GBP 80 per student to ensure that schools have the sufficient resources to help all students make up for lost teaching time. Special education institutions, or alternative settings for children unable to attend mainstream school due to exclusion from education, illness or other reasons, receive GBP 240 per student for the academic year. Schools will receive funds in three instalments across the academic year and are encouraged to pool funds to prioritise support according to student need. Schools should implement specific activities in line with both guidance on curriculum expectations for the next academic year and the Education Endowment Foundation's evidence-based support guide for schools and quick guide to implementation (Department for Education, United Kingdom, 2020[33]).

England (United Kingdom) National Tutoring Programme

To target support towards disadvantaged and vulnerable students specifically, England has allocated GBP 350 million for a National Tutoring Programme. This decision is based on extensive high-quality evidence demonstrating the potential of one-on-one and small-group tuition, delivered in partnership with schools, as a cost-effective way to support pupils who are falling behind. For primary and lower-secondary students, this entails the provision of high-quality tuition from November. The Department for Education will curate a list of approved tuition partners, from which schools can select the appropriate service. The Education Endowment Foundation is supporting the implementation of this programme, including impact evaluation. Schools in the most deprived areas will employ in-house academic mentors to provide small-group tuition. Teach First is leading the recruitment, initial and ongoing training, and placement of these mentors, who are likely to be graduates with some experience in education or of working with pupils. Some may be working towards an initial teacher training qualification. Both types of provision will be subsidised by the government, and schools can allocate further funding from the Catch-Up Premium to these programmes. For students in upper secondary and vocational education, schools can provide small group tutoring activities (Department for Education, United Kingdom, 2020[33]).

Wales (United Kingdom): Recruitment of extra teachers and teaching assistants

Wales is recruiting 600 extra teachers and 300 additional teaching assistants throughout the academic year 2020/21. These additional staff will be directed towards supporting students at the end of upper secondary school, as well as disadvantaged and vulnerable learners of all ages. This will support learners taking national end-of-cycle examinations in 2021 and those known to have been affected most while many schools have been closed since March. Professional learning resources will be provided to support new and existing teachers. Staff will be recruited on a one-year fixed-term contract and are expected to move into educational roles in the following school year. The support package, provided at a school level, could include extra coaching support, personalised learning programmes, and additional time and resources for exam year pupils (Welsh Government, 2020[34]).

Annex 11. Recent work from the OECD's Strength through Diversity project in the context of the COVID-19 pandemic

The OECD's Strength through Diversity: Education for Inclusive Societies project aims to identify how education systems can be equitable and inclusive by supporting the learning and well-being outcomes of diverse populations, and ensuring that all individuals are able to engage with others in increasingly diverse and complex societies.

This box provides an insight into a key relevant finding of the project during the COVID-19 crisis. It offers further substantive background to the Education Policy Reform Dialogues 2020 Session 1 – *Schools, higher education and Vocational Education and Training (VET): Making the most of resilient approaches in education for a better new normal*

Box 6. The Strength through Diversity Project's work on COVID-19

A focus on students' well-being

During the COVID-19 pandemic, the Strength through Diversity project has focused its work on the impact that the crisis has been having on vulnerable and disadvantaged students. Specifically it has produced several blog pieces on vulnerable groups (such as immigrant and refugee students, students with special education needs and Roma students)[1] and a forthcoming Brief titled "The impact of COVID-19 on student equity and inclusion: supporting vulnerable students during school closures and school re-openings". The Brief describes a range of current and potential practices to support vulnerable students during the pandemic, including the ones that focus on well-being.

The COVID-19 pandemic has highlighted that schools do not only have the role of education provider, but are also crucial to support the well-being of vulnerable students, since well-being conditions are closely linked to academic performance. In organising the return to school or forms of hybrid schooling, education systems should take into account their students' psychological health to ensure a safe transition back to school, or provide support in case of further lockdowns. Vulnerable students are more at a risk of being impacted in both their academic results and well-being outcomes by the current pandemic, and should be targeted by specific initiatives. It is thus important to consider what other provisions and extra services schools can offer to vulnerable students who might have been abused physically and psychologically, have not eaten or slept well, and might have experienced grief in the course of the pandemic. While many students might welcome the return to school, others may be feeling anxious or frightened.

Providing students with qualified psychological support could be a challenge for countries, both due to organisational obstacles and financial constraints during this crisis. However, training teachers and school personnel to respond effectively to students' fears and to communicate in an age-appropriate way can be key in fostering well-being upon school reopening. In France, for instance, the Ministry of Education provided resources and advice for teachers, including guidelines targeting students with special education needs who may have already struggled with their mental health, and several resources to inform the youngest on the virus and how to protect their health and that of their families. In England (United Kingdom), too, teachers are instructed to use "well-being guides" to help children understand what is occurring due to the pandemic and talk about their feelings. Supporting teachers in the efforts to foster students' well-being is a key policy area in promoting the resilience and responsiveness of education systems while the COVID-19 crisis takes place and possibly also during its aftermath.

Note: 1. Blog pieces from the Strength through Diversity project are available here: https://oecdedutoday.com/.

Sources: (Ministère de l"Éducation Nationale et de la Jeunesse et des Sports, 2020[35]), "Welcoming all students to school and college", *News – Pedagogical Continuity*, webpage of Eduscol, France, https://eduscol.education.fr/cid151499/reouverture-des-ecoles.html (accessed on 13 October 2020); (OECD, n.d.[36]), "The impact of COVID-19 on student equity and inclusion: supporting vulnerable students during school closures and school re-openings", *OECD Policy Responses to Coronavirus (COVID-19)*; (Shoffman, 2020[37]), "How English primary schools are focusing on emotional education to reopen safely during the coronavirus pandemic", webpage, Business Insider France, https://www.businessinsider.fr/us/english-schools-focusing-mental-health-while-reopening-during-covid-19-2020-6 (accessed on 13 October 2020).

For further information please visit: http://www.oecd.org/education/strength-through-diversity/.